Acclaim

Freeing the Artistic Mind

Master Class - Based Upon This Book

Life reaches out to you at the craziest times in the most wonderful ways. For the past few weeks, I have been lost and searching for guidance. When Dr. Crawford came and talked to us, I felt like he had specifically designed this lecture for my life. Obviously, he had not, but what he had to say, the advice he had to give was so relevant to my life that it felt personalized. I sat in that room absolutely infatuated with what he had to say and the wisdom he gave us. I think that his class is one that should be heard by people everywhere. I feel inspired to change my life, to change my connections, to connect deeper, to let go of things and people causing me pain, and to realize fully the important aspects of my life. I say thank you, thank you, thank you to Dr. Crawford for being patient, wonderful, and inspiring. This class truly changed my life, and I don't say that often. The world functions in crazy ways! - Elizabeth Brady, Texas State University

Dr. Crawford, What a remarkable job you did over the past two days - holding the attention of an entire school and talking with all our students so openly and with such care. It was clear from the student's reaction at the end of today's session what a positive impact you made on them. Thank you so very much for your inspiring words, your step by step method, and your sensitive and supportive guidance . I look forward very much to hearing how your work with the younger generations of artists continues.
Barbara MacKenzie-Wood
Raymond W. Smith Professor of Drama

School of Drama
Carnegie Mellon University

I'm so happy that Dr. Crawford came to do a master class! It was so different than anything I have been exposed to, and it was something that I think is really pertinent to actors, considering the demanding nature of our field. I really hope we have the opportunity to collaborate with him again in the near future!! - Emma Hearn, Texas State University

Dr. Crawford has given me an invaluable gift—a way to communicate with my students and help them deal with things they are struggling with on a daily basis. I am a better teacher and a more effective mentor because of what I've learned from Bill Crawford.
Jim Price
Head of Dramatic Writing
Texas State University

Hi Dr. Crawford! - First and foremost, I want to say thank you very much for coming out tonight to Rider University. I know the weather was less than ideal, but I think your presence at tonight's theater lab was one for the books. I think that what you did in a very short amount of time will help me live a higher quality life. In the past, I have found myself annoyed, angry, or jealous constantly! The idea of a having a higher purpose of something you yourself have control over and is part of a process of becoming the person you want to be is so much more helpful then just acknowledging the problem, moving on, and hoping it doesn't happen again. Dr. Crawford, there's not much I can say about your presentation as far as improvement. I can't think of any questions I have at the moment, but I hope to read some of your books in the future, and I think your name will be a present one in the Rider community from here on out.
Hannah Cohen, Rider University

On Saturday, September 6th, 2014, my life was changed. Dr. Bill Crawford came in and handed me the essentials to living life on a silver platter. As an 18 year old freshman who struggles with time management, stress has been a familiar plague that I thought was always going to be a part of my life. I had accepted that I would never outgrow those frantic episodes of panic where my judgement blurred and everything seemed to be caving in. But Dr. Crawford disagreed. He laid out a simple, step by step process on how to get your mind to slow down and think rationally, asserting that stress was not in the situation, but in my brain's way of receiving information. He presented a series of four questions that, due to their simple complexity, would actually require my neocortex to activate and answer, putting my rash brainstem out of a job! And, once the new habits have been formed, I can think more clearly about how to manage my time, reducing the amount of triggers, and, in turn, reducing the chance of being stressed. It's an upward spiral! - Anna Uzele, Texas State University

Dr. Crawford,
I wanted to THANK YOU for the amazing gift you gave to our Musical Theater students at Rider University with your workshop on stress and life. The student's responses the next day in class were so positive. It was also reconfirming that the workshop you gave was important not just to our students, but also our faculty. It opened so many conversations between the students and faculty. Inspiring, fun, informative... a necessity for any young artists, and especially helpful to our young artists in school. Looking forward to your new book and how your research continues. Thank you,
 Robin Lewis, Musical Theater
Head of Theater and Dance
Westminster College of the Arts at Rider University

I had a mind-blowing experience in Dr. Crawford's master class this past weekend. I kept telling everyone that it is the One Voice of stress relief because it was so revolutionary, but made so much sense at the same time. I was so amazed to learn why we get stuck in our brainstem, then find it nearly impossible to move into our neocortex. In addition, I found it so interesting that the neocortex is responsible for so many important traits, one of which is creativity. This really resonated with me because I have struggled with my creativity and confidence in certain types of auditions. I also really appreciate Dr Crawford taking the time to understand what we go through with respect to auditions, rehearsals, and callbacks on top of all of our school work!- Julia Estrada, Texas State University*

After Dr. Crawford's visit, I find myself being able to fall back asleep in the middle of the night much more easily. I've also always had a hard time with roommates and difficult people, and I've found myself dealing with those situations better and trying to follow the steps Dr. Crawford has given us. I see now how I can change that for myself, and what I can work on to keep that positivity going! I really loved this masterclass, and I find myself constantly thinking about it whenever I'm feeling stressed or stuck in a negative situation! Thank you, Dr. Crawford. Taylor Jackson, Rider University

So, I think I can speak for most of us when I say this workshop was NEEDED at this time in our lives. For my sake, I am moving into a brand new apartment, have a brand new load of responsibilities on my hands, dealing with quite a lot of change, and have felt swamped day after day in stress. My point is, I needed help. Advice that I could not only understand, but truly connect with and APPLY in my life. And, I needed it as fast as possible. Because knowing myself well enough, I would never reach out to anyone for fear of appearing weak. So, what did I take from it? It's all science. Once we can acknowledge that, and see past the idea that "we cannot change," that "this is what has been given to us and there is nothing we can do," then we can LEARN HOW TO IMPROVE! It's not what you are stopping, it's what your are STARTING. We have a lot of power to influence who we want to be.- Maggie Bera, Texas State University

"When I first invited Dr. Bill Crawford to speak to the theater department at Texas State, I knew there was a real need for students in the arts to learn better ways to manage their stress and anxiety. What I couldn't imagine, however, was the powerful impact this master class would have on our students, and even our program. Not only were the students thoroughly engaged from the beginning, to this day they continue to rave at how much they learned, and the degree to which this material has not only helped them deal with stress, but actually changed their lives. I want to personally thank Dr. Crawford for sharing his unique philosophy with our students and faculty, and I applaud his efforts to support other programs and young artists around the country."
Laura Lane
Head of Acting
Texas State University

The master class that happened this past weekend was simply life changing. I feel like I'm already approaching the way I handle stress completely differently, and it hasn't even been a week since the class. I felt like I really understood everything he was trying to get across, and I really want to work hard to apply it to my life. I have been feeling extremely stressed out lately, so this master class could not have come at a better time for me. It felt as if it were meant for me to hear, and I cannot even express how much I've taken away from this experience. I think one of the reasons why it was so amazing was because of how passionate

Dr. Crawford is for his job. I really do feel like this way of thinking could work simply because of how passionate he was about this idea. It is definitely a master class that I will never forget! Chelsi Jump, Texas State University

Dear Dr. Crawford - You changed my life. That's the simplest and most forward way that I can put it. I have been obsessing for the past few months on concepts relating to your teachings, but I couldn't find a way to articulate what I was thinking and feeling. Your seminar put it perfectly and was so accessible! The only thing I enjoyed as much as what you taught was the way you taught, with vivacity and passion that made me want to hear what you had to say. I have been implementing the four questions in my life every day and figuring out what is my highest purpose and realizing that it is always changing! Nevertheless, Thank you so much, and I only pray that you come again. - John Brantley III

Listening to Dr. Bill Crawford speak to us this Saturday was four of the most valuable hours I've spent in college to date. I loved the way Dr. Crawford spoke to us. He was very open and friendly. I instantly felt at ease around him and willing to open myself up. I always feel like my stress is emotion-based, but hearing how it's actually a chemical change in your body makes me feel strangely better. One of the most valuable lessons I'm taking away from this experience is the notion of "what are you teaching to those you love?" To me that really sums it up. If I'm stressed or upset or frustrated and letting those emotions out in a negative way, I need to stop and ask myself that question. Would I teach this to my loved ones? I need to treat myself with the same respect that I would give to them. I gained a lot from this master class. I'm so grateful that Dr. Crawford spent the time and energy to come talk to us. Incredibly worthwhile! - Adria Swan, Texas State University

FREEING
THE
ARTISTIC
MIND

FREEING THE ARTISTIC MIND

A Student's Guide to Greater Clarity, Confidence, & Creativity

Bill Crawford, Ph.D.

Florence Publishing
Houston, Tx

Manufactured in the United States of America
Cover Graphics by Rebecca Cook
Text Graphics: Created by Bill Crawford and Georgia Crawford with additional illustrations by Dover Publications, Inc., Tim Teebeken of Artville, L.L.C.,

Library of Congress Control Number: 2015912698
ISBN: 978-0-9653461-4-6

Bill Crawford, Ph.D.
Crawford Performance Solutions
1-888-530-8550
Email - DrBill@billcphd.com
Website - www.billcphd.com

To my wife, Georgia,
and my sons, Chris and Nik
with all my love.

Acknowledgements

Each time I attempt a project as all-encompassing as writing a book, I am reminded of how much the talents and contributions of others play an integral part in creating the final product. I am grateful for the opportunity to thank these individuals for their support.

Let me begin close to home and start by thanking my wife, Georgia, for her support, patience, and enthusiasm for this project. Not only did she spend many a sleepless night proofing and making changes in the final manuscript, she did this while continuing her multi-generational role as loving mother to our two sons, Christopher and Nicholas, and loving daughter to her mother, Mrs. Socrates Rombakis. I am continually amazed at how having her as a relationship partner has enriched my life, and allowed me to do the work that I do from a foundation of love. Further, not only has she been a significant factor in the creation of this foundation, she continues to be an example of the power of love as a resource for recreating a sense of family on a daily basis.

Let me also thank my two sons, Christopher and

Nicholas (or Chris and Nik as they prefer). They continue to be a reminder of the importance of being purposeful in my role as a father so that I am always mindful of responding to life in a way that I would be proud for them to emulate.

In fact, this book that is focused on young artists, is the result of watching Nik grow in his love for performing, and coming to understand the stress that he and his friends deal with. He was gracious enough to share the spotlight with me at Texas State University, and this experience led me to revise my philosophy to support young people in the performing and visual arts.

In fact, it was the enthusiastic response I received from the students and facuty at Texas State that has motivated me to write this book, and do everything I can to support young artists. Specifically, I want to thank Kaitlin Hopkins (Head of Musical Theater at Texas State) and Jim Price (Head of Playwriting) for their friendship and support. These are very special people who demonstrate their devotion to their students and their craft in every aspect of their lives. To have individuals such as Kaitlin and Jim supporting me and my work has been, and continues to be, such a meaningful experience. They were gracious enough to write the foreword to this book, and their willingness to recommend me and my work to others has been a significant factor in my success in this new endeavor to date.

Finally, I would like to thank my mother and father, Florence and Burton Crawford. Even though they passed away over 40 years ago, I am touched daily by their warmth, love, and philosophy of life. Their commitment to creating a loving home for me, as well as helping others through the programs of A.A. and Alanon has given me a foundation on which to build a life and a life's work. In many ways, they live on in every word of this book.

Contents

Part I

Part II

Foreword

Kaitlin Hopkins & Jim Price

We met Dr. Bill Crawford in September of 2014. He was visiting our Texas State University campus to give a master class for our students on how to deal with stress, difficult people, and just as importantly, how to make decisions in our lives that actually serve us. That workshop changed the majority of our students' lives, as well as our own. It especially impacted our freshmen, who, like many college freshmen around the country, were trying so hard to fit in to their new environment. Many of them reported feeling confused and lost because they didn't have the tools to navigate through this new, independent world on their own. The college environment presents unique challenges at every turn—time management issues in the face of a crushing workload, identity issues, relationships, sex, as well as an exposure to drugs and alcohol--some for the first time.

For students at all levels, Bill's message couldn't have come at a better time. It was completely accessible, immediately implementable, and it has become a foundational element in much of what we teach our students today. It has given us a common vocabulary to communicate with students when they are in trouble, and we have been thrilled to see the students already use this new language to help each other. With all the progress we've made dealing with so many of the above issues, it's hard to believe Dr. Crawford only came into our lives seven months ago.

We both feel very strongly that, as educators in the performing arts, we have a responsibility to not only teach our students how to act, sing, and dance well, but to also give them tools to help them live in the world as healthy humans—physically, vocally, emotionally, holistically. We all have it in our curricula to train our students to do triple pirouettes, to sing from the soul, to personalize each and every acting moment they encounter in a scene or monologue, but what about when they leave the rigors of the rehearsal room—what then?

We were spending a lot of time educating our students in their chosen profession and covering all aspects of acting, singing and dancing. We were teaching them everything from how to be a professional, to the business of our business, to health and nutrition as it related to their vocal instruments and their bodies. But we were giving them little or no information about how to deal with basic life problems--we weren't giving them the coping skills and tools needed for success in the business in a sustainable way. We both realized that there was a missing element to the training our students were getting.

This book has come at just the right time. It is something we can introduce into our program's curriculum that will help our students to practice healthy decision making, lead them down the pathway to a more stress-free existence, and help them create and maintain better relationships, even with difficult people they encounter along the way. It helps them access the upper, more creative part of their brain (the neocortex) on a consistent basis, all the while leading them away from the fear-based, lower part of their brain (the brainstem). Dr. Crawford's approach has been revelatory for our students-- we're not only seeing it translate into a healthier, more creative approach to work in the classroom and on stage, but we're also seeing the powerful effect it's having on the way our students live their lives. They now understand how their brain processes information, and this new understanding helps guide them through the tough times and makes them feel more in control of their lives and less trapped by their stress.

For almost thirty years, Bill Crawford has traveled the world helping CEO's, health care professionals, and those working in corporations access their clarity, confidence and creativity. His son, Nik is now pursuing a BFA degree in acting here at Texas State, and as a result, Bill has turned his focus in our direction, and we are so grateful that he has.

There are more degree programs in the performing arts than ever before. There are more hopeful students enrolling in these programs than ever before with greater competition across the board. This book goes way beyond "stress management." Freeing the Artistic Mind gives young artists the information and the tools they need to navigate the world of performing arts training in a clear, confident, and creative way. It frees them to explore who they are as individuals as they develop their own unique artistic voice on the way to defining a new generation of creative artists. As professionals who have worked closely with Dr. Crawford and witnessed the impact of this material first hand, we can't recommend this book highly enough.

Kaitlin Hopkins
Head of Musical Theatre
Texas State University

Jim Price
Head of Drramatic Writing
Texas State University

March 8, 2015

Introduction

As books go, I'm proud to say that this is my fifth. My first two on *stress* and *dealing with difficult people,* were written in conjunction with the two PBS specials that I had the pleasure to film in Houston, and later make available to the nationwide PBS network.

My fourth book was entitled, "Life from the Top of the Mind." This was my "flagship" book, meaning that it contained my entire philosophy on dealing with stress, difficult people, and bringing one's best to life, regardless of the situation.

I say all of this to give you some sense of how this book might be similar to, and yet different from my previous works. The similarity is that the "Life from the Top of the Mind" models I use in all of my books have remained intact, and I have also incorporated some of the examples I used in previous works to illustrate how to apply the material to real life. However, what makes this book different is that this is the first time I have attempted to combine all that I know into a comprehensive guide for young artists.

As you have read in the Acknowledgements and the Foreword, all of this came about as a result of a master class I did for the theater department at

Texas State University.

Even though it was an all-day affair, the students (about 100 of them, from both acting and musical theater) were ravenous in their desire to learn and make use of this new material. They were eager and engaged, and weren't afraid to go deep with their questions and self-disclosure. In a few short months, this enthusiastic response was then replicated at Carnegie Mellon, The Musical Theater Educator's Alliance Conference (MTEA) in New York City, Rider University, and The Relativity School in Los Angeles. In addition, future master classes are scheduled for the 2015/2016 academic year at Otterbein, Ohio Northern, Shenandoah, and NYU.

As a result of this success, Kaitlin, Jim, and I are wanting to make this material available to young artists everywhere, and we hope this book will play a large role in making this a reality.

In terms of how the book is organized, all of the material and models presented are developmental in nature, meaning that each new concept not only addresses a specific block to success, but also builds on what has already been presented, and further, lays a foundation for what's to come.

Part One describes why the book is necessary, or how problematic situations can trigger certain reactions which create an increasingly debilitating cycle that blocks our ability to succeed. Once this process has been explained, I go on to offer a powerful solution that can be applied immediately.

Part Two builds on these concepts, and presents a series of additional models designed to make the change permanent. Both Part One and Two are about how to deal with problematic situations such as auditions, school, relationships, fear of the future, etc. Part Three is devoted to applying all that has been presented to dealing with difficult people, and/or becoming more influential in your interactions with others. Part Four will tie everything together, and give you some suggestions on what to do next in order to become skilled at bringing this "Top of the Mind" perspective to life.

My sincere wish is that you will find this book valuable, and that as a result of reading and working with the models presented, you are able to become more influential in your life and your work. Or, put another way, that this material will free you to be who you are and do what you love for the rest of your life.

Part I

CHAPTER I

The Problem

Debbie is an 18 year old freshman musical theater major at a prestigious performing arts program. She has been stressing over being accepted into a good program for over a year, and now that she is in, she is stressed about measuring up to everyone's expectations. She is away from home for the first time and feels overwhelmed by classes and dorm life, and wonders if she will ever feel like she belongs.

Damian is a senior acting major, and despite being praised for his work over the last two years, he is terrified about life after college. Where should he go... LA, New York, Chicago? Or maybe he should just forget about trying to make it as an actor, and get a real job like his father keeps telling him. On top of all this, his girlfriend thinks she may be pregnant!

Julie is a sophomore who, despite multiple auditions and callbacks, has yet to be cast in a mainstage production. She is beginning to question whether she is meant to pursue this career, and this anxiety is manifesting into an eating disorder. She knows she should get help with this, but she is afraid of being seen as weak.

What all of these people have in common is that none of them are living the life they envisioned. While all of their problems and reactions are under-standable, the result is that they become increasingly overwhelmed, anxious, confused, and frustrated. Unfortunately, this only makes their problems seem worse, which then triggers another round of stress, frustration, and anxiety, and they become caught in a cycle, or downward spiral that I call "The Cycle of Stress/Frustration."

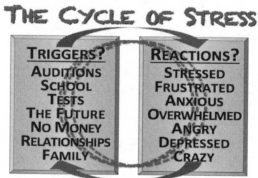

THE CYCLE OF STRESS

TRIGGERS?	REACTIONS?
AUDITIONS	STRESSED
SCHOOL	FRUSTRATED
TESTS	ANXIOUS
THE FUTURE	OVERWHELMED
NO MONEY	ANGRY
RELATIONSHIPS	DEPRESSED
FAMILY	CRAZY

Sound familiar? Are there aspects of your life that are triggering certain reactions and throwing you into your own cycle? If so, then regardless of whether you are a performing artist or visual artist, you have come to the right place. My purpose in writing this book is to give you a clear understanding of why this stress and anxiety seems to be so prevalent, and more importantly, what can be done. In other words, a step-by-step guide to bringing your best to life, even (and maybe especially) in the most difficult of situations.

Before we go any further, I want to emphasize that this is not just another book on "stress management." I'm not going to suggest that taking a deep breath and chanting, "Don't worry, be happy" is the solution to your dilemma. It has been my experience that most people are tired of simplistic answers to life's complex problems. Thus, I will not insult you by telling you what you already know, or that "you've had the answer all along." In fact, I believe that it is just this tendency to try to solve our problems using incomplete information that has resulted in an increase in our stress and frustration. Or, as Albert Einstein says:

"Problems cannot be solved at the same level of awareness that created them."

This means that if we don't have a good understanding (sufficient level of awareness) of what stress and anxiety really are, as well as what is truly creating the cycle, our attempt to address what isn't working won't work. In other words, when we see our stress (frustration, anxiety, depression) as the problem, and the external triggers as the cause of the problem, we naturally try to change the cause. Unfortunately, because so many of the negative aspects of our lives are not under our direct control (auditions, the future, other people, etc.) the result is that we feel more, stressed, frustrated, anxious, angry, overwhelmed, etc., and the infamous cycle is created and maintained.

Now, just to be clear, I'm not one of those people in the field of psychology that says you have no right to feel this way, or even that you are wrong for feeling angry or frustrated. I just want you to ask yourself one question . . .

How's it working for you? !!!

I ask this question because most people would say, "IT'S NOT!," meaning that they don't want to go around feeling stressed, angry, anxious, frustrated, overwhelmed, or stressed. And, couldn't we easily add "resentful" to the list of reactions? Don't most people resent having to deal with all of these problems all of the time? If so, there is a great quote about "resentment" that might serve us well in our plan to regain control:

"Resentment is like taking poison and waiting for the other person to die!"
Malachy McCourt

I find this quote valuable because it succinctly captures what is going on here. We are feeling understandably resentful of the negative situations that seem to be causing our problems. However, we also seem to be trying to use this resentment as motivation to solve the problem. Unfortunately, all that does is poison our system with certain chemicals (more on this later), and set us up to feel bad, lose focus, and make mistakes.

I remember a time when I was caught in one of these cycles of resentment and stress. It began innocently enough. I was just sitting in an airport waiting to catch a plane to my next speaking engagement. I was thinking about where I was about to go and what I wanted to say when an announcement came over the speaker system stating that my flight had been canceled. This was years before I had perfected my current method of handling such events, and thus I started to become stressed and worried about what I was going to do. Then I noticed that there were very few people waiting to catch this flight, and I began to wonder if they had canceled the flight because there were not enough passengers to make the trip profitable. Now, in addition to feeling stressed and worried, I became angry and resentful, and I was just about to give those airline people a piece of my mind when . . . "mother nature" called. Of course, as we all know, this is a call that cannot be ignored, and so, oblivious to pretty much everyone and everything around me, I stormed off to the bathroom rehearsing what I was going to say to the people at the airline counter.

As it turns out, the bathroom was empty, and so I picked a stall, sat down, and was continuing to practice my tirade when . . . someone in a pair of high heels walked in! One would think that this would bring me back to reality with a distinct crash, however, I was so caught up in being "right," I just assumed that everyone else was wrong, and therefore she must have wandered into the wrong bathroom. I didn't want to embarrass her (for after all, it wasn't her fault that the flight was cancelled) and so I was trying to think of a polite way to let her know of her mistake when . . . another person wearing women's shoes walked in! Of course, at that moment I realized that I WAS IN THE WRONG BATHROOM!!! Further, if I said something now, it would have looked like I had been hiding in there all along.

As you might imagine, all thoughts and emo-

tions concerning the cancelled flight disappeared
and were replaced by worries about my current
predicament. I remembered that no one was in the
bathroom when I first came in, and thus decided that
if I just covered my eyes and didn't make a sound,
they would eventually leave and I could escape.
Well, about that time a plane must have landed because the place filled up, and I knew that sooner or
later someone was going to notice my shoes or just
want the stall, and thus the "wait them out" solution was no longer viable. So, mustering all of my
courage, I said "Excuse me" and the place got really
quiet. Next, I said, "I am not a pervert, this was a
mistake, and if everyone will just cover up, I will
leave." I then proceeded to exit the bathroom, hand
over my eyes, attempting to be as inconspicuous as
possible, but having very little success.

How could this happen? Well, clearly I was
so angry and stressed about the cancelled flight that
I didn't pay attention to whether the figure on the
door of the bathroom was wearing pants or a skirt
(not to mention failing to read the sign!) In addition,
I was so worried about the original mistake that I
compounded it by trying to avoid taking responsibility for my error in judgment.

While hopefully you will never find your-
self in this situation, I think it's fair to say that the
process of reacting to our triggers with more stress
is a familiar experience for most of us, and further,
the ensuing cycle is something we would all like to

avoid. If so, then I suggest that we draw upon the wisdom of Dr. Einstein, and raise our awareness of what is truly happening in these situations.

CHAPTER 2

The Natural Law of Cycles

The first thing that we need to understand is that there is a natural law operating here, and if we are not aware of this law, we may unwittingly use it against ourselves. I call it the "Natural Law of Cycles," which basically states that all of life presents itself as a cycle of cause and effect. In terms of our thoughts and emotions, most people see "the cause" as what makes us feel something and, of course, when this is positive, there is no problem. However, when what we perceive as "the cause" is negative (auditions, deadlines, an uncertain future. etc.), then *we* become "the effect," and *that* is a problem.

WE BECOME THE EFFECT!

TRIGGERS?	REACTIONS?
AUDITIONS	STRESSED
SCHOOL	FRUSTRATED
TESTS	ANXIOUS
THE FUTURE	OVERWHELMED
NO MONEY	ANGRY
RELATIONSHIPS	DEPRESSED
FAMILY	CRAZY

When this is the case, there are three ways to change:

1. Change the cause: On some level, this is what most people attempt first, meaning that when they feel angry, frustrated, or stressed, most people try to fix the problem by changing what they believe made them upset, and if this is possible, I think it's a great idea. In other words, if you can influence your environment in such a way that results in your feeling better, then by all means give it your best shot. However, most people find that there are many aspects of life that either resist our efforts to change them, or are just beyond our control. When this is the case, attempting to change the cause only "causes" more stress.

2. Change the effect: The second option involving the natural law of cycles is more powerful, however, it is certainly a road less traveled, because most people don't even think it's possible. It describes dealing with the cycle of cause and effect by changing the effect. This involves changing how difficult situations affect us by choosing how we want to respond. Most "self-help" books advocate this approach, and while it is certainly a wonderful skill to have, it is also limited in that no matter how accomplished we become, we are still the effect. This is why I advocate an even more rare, and in some ways, more radical approach I call "becoming the cause."

3. Become the cause: As mentioned, this third option is even more unorthodox than the first two, and thus it is even more rare. However, I believe that this is the most powerful way to harness the natural law of cycles and deal with the cycle of stress/frustration. In short, rather than advising you to spend your energies trying to change the situation (especially when it is not within your control) or even change the effect, I am suggesting that you flip the cycle and become "the cause," or become the most powerful, influential person in your life, which is what this book is all about.

CHAPTER 3

Changing Stress from the Problem to the Solution

In order to adopt this more powerful perspective (becoming the cause), we must also raise our awareness of the true nature of the problem. In other words, in addition to the Natural Law of Cycles, another aspect of the problem that we need to understand more fully is what "stress" (frustration, anxiety, confusion, etc.) really is, and how we can become more influential with respect to this aspect of our lives.

Interestingly enough, our lack of understanding around this issue doesn't stem from a lack of exposure. You can't turn around without seeing a new book or magazine article about the subject of stress. However, as promised, I am not going to rehash this information or tell you what you already know. In fact, unlike most people who talk about stress, I'm going to suggest that stress isn't even the problem, but actually part of the solution! A quote that I use in my presentations which speaks to this perspective states that:

"Stress is a signal that something needs to change . . . Suffering is when we don't make the change."

I like this way of looking at the subject because it defines stress not as the problem, but rather as a valuable signal that when ignored can lead to the real problem... suffering. For example, imagine you are moving your hand closer and closer to a hot stove. (Kids, don't try this at home!) You will begin to feel "stress" in the form of heat and pain. THAT'S THE GOOD NEWS! If you didn't feel this signal, you would destroy your hand. In this case, "stress" is a valuable signal, and when seen as such, can become part of the solution.

Another good example are the warning lights on the dashboard of a car. Let's assume that we are driving down the road, and one of these warning lights become illuminated.

If we dealt with that light the way most of us deal with stress (i.e., saw it as the problem), we might become annoyed and want to reach over, break it out, and keep on driving, thinking, "There, now everything is fine." Of course, we don't do this because the little red light isn't the problem...it's part of the solution! It lets us know that something needs our attention. By the way, have you noticed how much more attention we pay to the warning lights on our dashboard versus the warning signals from our body?

Bottom line, stress isn't what we have been told it is. It isn't what someone or something does to us. ("Auditions really stress me out," or "Deadlines just drive me crazy") nor is it our failure to cope ("What's wrong with me? "Why do I let all of this get to me?")

What we call "stress" is really just a series of chemical reactions in our brain and body!

I am putting extra emphasis on this statement for two reasons. One, this concept is the foundation for much of the material we will discuss from this point on, and two, this is a relatively new take on the problem.

In fact, in the not too distant past, if you wanted to find out how stressed someone was, you would give them a test. This would consist of a list of life experiences (such as death of a loved one, divorce, job loss, a major move, etc.) and each experience would be assigned a weight or number. The idea was that if enough bad things were happening to you in life, your number would be high, and you would be described as suffering from "stress."

The problem was that not everyone with high numbers described themselves as stressed, while many people who didn't have scores in the problematic range reported being "very stressed." What researchers came to realize is that there had to be other factors operating here, and they began to explore what happens chemically in our brain and body during these experiences. They discovered that there are three major chemicals associated with the experience of being "stressed." These are adrenaline, noradrenaline, and cortisol. Of the three, cortisol is the most important.

In fact, measuring how much cortisol is in one's blood stream or saliva is now one way to determine how "stressed" someone is. Of course, this isn't to say that these chemicals are all bad. In fact, if we look at the relationship between stress and productivity, we find that when there is zero stress in our lives, there is zero productivity. . .

It's called sleep! The truth is that we are not very productive when we are sleeping! Plus, when we are sleeping, there is very little adrenaline, noradrenaline, and cortisol in our body. In fact, guess what chemicals wake us up in the morning? You guessed it, adrenaline, noradrenaline, and cortisol.

So, for a while in the morning, as our stress goes up in the form of these chemicals, our productivity goes up as well. We are more productive three hours after we wake up than we are three minutes after we wake up, and that's because we have these chemicals going throughout our body.

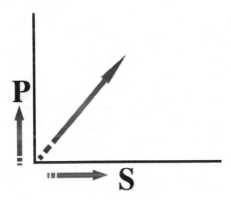

However, as most of us have experienced, as our stress continues to go up, at some point our productivity goes down, and eventually we crash and burn (or experience burnout).

Therefore, following Dr. Einstein's suggestion that the more awareness we bring to a situation, the more successful we will be, I want to help you become aware of when you first feel pushed over the top and begin that all too familiar downward spiral. Then, because stress is just a series of chemical reactions in your body, I want to show you how to use stress as a valuable signal, and actually CHANGE THE CHEMICAL MAKEUP OF YOUR BODY so that you can bring yourself back into your zone of productivity.

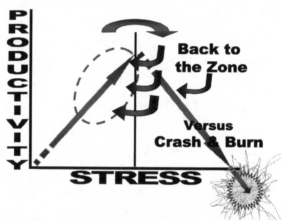

By the way, when I am talking about "productivity" here, I'm not just referring to being productive at school or work. I'm talking about bringing our best to any aspect of life. Plus, I'm not here to tell you where you "should" be with respect to your productivity. You can bring yourself back at a high level, medium level, or low level. That is up to you. I just want to show you how you can be more influential in this process, versus be controlled by the negative aspects of life.

Okay, now we know about the Natural Law of Cycles, and the fact that what we have been calling "stress" is actually a series of chemical changes in our body. In order to become more influential in this process, we must also understand how all of this works in our brains (which will also shed more light on just what I mean by "Freeing The Artistic Mind," or living "Life from the Top of the Mind.")

Most people know that our brains are divided into three parts: the brainstem, the limbic system, and the neocortex.

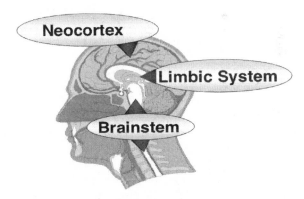

The brainstem (the lower part of the brain) is where our fight-or-flight responses are located, and is also the part of the brain that regulates our breathing, heart rate, blood pressure, and muscle tension. The middle of our brain is called the limbic system, and this is where our emotions are triggered. However, this middle brain also acts as a gatekeeper. Or, in today's terminology, it acts as a scanner, a processor, and a router. It scans incoming data, processes it or interprets it, and either routes it down to the brain-stem or up to the upper 80% of our brain called the neocortex, where we have access to our interpersonal skills, problem-solving skills, clarity, confidence, creativity, compassion, etc.

Here's how all of this works. Data comes in from our five senses, and it is first scanned by the limbic system. If the limbic system determines that there is no problem (for example, at the moment you are reading this book), then the data is sent up to the neocortex, the brainstem works in the background regulating our breathing, heart rate, blood pressure, etc., and all is well. However, if the limbic system senses any problem, anything or anyone it doesn't like, anything or anyone that it has identified as a problem, a stressor, a trigger or a threat of any kind... or anything or anyone that is similar to any problem or threat it has experienced in the past, then it sends the information immediately down to the brainstem... **bypassing the neocortex!**

Of course, at this point, the brainstem can only respond in two ways: fight or flight, and so to prepare for this response, this lower part of the brain triggers the release of adrenaline, noradrenaline, and cortisol, which results in an increase of our heart rate, muscle tension, blood pressure, etc.

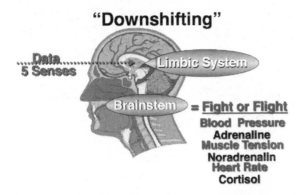

"Downshifting"

In the latest brain research, this is called "downshifting" because it happens so fast, and again, for our purposes, what is important is how this process **bypasses the most intelligent, purposeful, creative part of our brain (the neocortex)!**

Now, to be clear, I'm not saying that this is always a bad thing. In fact, in a true fight-or-flight situation, this is exactly what you want to happen. For example, imagine you are walking down the street and someone jumps out from the bushes. You certainly wouldn't want to have to stand there and think about the situation or your response . . . "Hmmmm, someone just jumped out from the bushes . . . wonder what I should do?" No, in this sort of situation, an immediate fight-or-flight reaction is clearly what is called for, and the good news is that evolution has set us up well for this reaction. Thousands of years of surviving saber-toothed tigers and other dangers has given us a brain and nervous system that reacts to perceived threats in a very specific way.

The bad news is that few (if any) of the problematic situations we encounter on a daily basis today actually call for a fight-or-flight response. Quite the opposite, they require our best problem-solving skills, interpersonal skills, confidence, and creativity in order for us to be successful.

Unfortunately, due to the limbic system hijacking the data and sending it down to our brainstem, we are now coming from the lower 20% of our brain, and producing chemicals that raise our heart rate, blood pressure, muscle tension, etc., and limit our ability to respond. (In his book, *Emotional Intelligence*, Daniel Goleman, calls this process "neural hijacking" or, "emotional hijacking")

Of course, when I say "fight-or-flight," I don't mean simply the tendency to either attack something or run away from it. The "fight" reaction can manifest as becoming defensive, argumentative, or rigid in one's position, while the "flight" can show up as depression, withdrawal, and/or avoidance.

Unfortunately, when we try to deal with the perceived problem from this limited part of the brain, we are often less than successful, which, of course, has us feeling even more powerless, frustrated, stressed, and anxious. The limbic system interprets these additional problematic feelings as even more negative data, and dutifully sends it right back down to the brainstem.

This triggers the production of even more adrenaline, noradrenaline, and cortisol, which results in a further increase in blood pressure, heart rate, and muscle tension, and the cycle of stress becomes our experience of life.

Trapped!

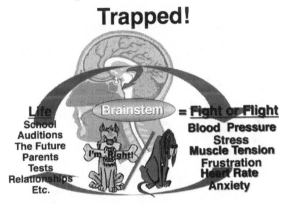

As you can see, the problem is that we are becoming trapped in the lower part of our brain which cannot solve the problem. In fact,

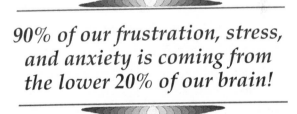

90% of our frustration, stress, and anxiety is coming from the lower 20% of our brain!

I call this part of the brain our "undermind" because not only is it physically under the rest of our brain, it's also where we feel undermined by the world around us. I also call it the "moat mentality" because this is where many people feel attacked, and start focusing all of their energy on defending themselves, their work, reputation, etc., by building moats or circling the wagons.

In addition to the "undermind" and the "moat mentality," another phrase I use to describe this situation is the "world of the underdog," because here is also where people tend to fall into one of two categories: Either they are fiercely holding on to the righteousness of their perspective, thinking and/or saying, "I'm Right!"or they feel undermined and defeated, and seem to be saying, "I give up. There is nothing I can do. What's the use?."

Whatever you call it, what's clear is that this lower part of the brain is no place to live. It doesn't work for Debbie, the MT student who is afraid of not measuring up. It doesn't work for Damian, the senior acting student who is afraid of the future. It doesn't work for Julie who is worried that she will never be chosen for a major part, and it doesn't work for you!

Therefore, rather than just showing you how to "manage stress" (i.e., keep it down to a manageable level), I am going to give you a model that will allow you to change the chemical makeup of your body, and shift from the lower 20% of the brain (the brainstem) and free your artistic mind to function at its best. Then, I'm going to give you another model that will help you stay in this clear, confident, and creative mind-set so that you can bring your best to whatever you are doing, and experience the power and promise of living "Life from the Top of the Mind."

CHAPTER 4

Regaining Control

If, after examining your life, you discover that you are finding yourself coming from your brainstem and feeling way more anxious, worried, and stressed than you would like , the good news is that shifting from the brainstem to the neocortex and changing the chemical makeup of your body isn't as daunting a task as it may sound. In fact, smokers do this all the time. Don't worry, I'm not going to recommend that you take up smoking in order to regain control of your life.

However, I do think it's interesting to note that every time I ask a smoker or former smoker the question, "Does or did smoking help you deal with stress?" they almost always answer "Yes!" When I ask seminar participants why this is, many say that it must have something to do with the chemicals that are being inhaled. However, nicotine, the principle chemical that is being ingested by smokers, is a stimulant! By all rights, those who use cigarettes should say that they are stimulated by the act of smoking, however most say that lighting up actually calms them down.

What could be happening here that is so powerful it overrides the effect of a chemical stimulant? First, smokers seem to be responding to a signal. They may be working on a particularly stressful project or deadline, and something clicks in their brain that says, "Man, I need a cigarette!" Next, they stop whatever they are doing and go out to the dumpster (because that's the only place we will let them smoke anymore) and begin their ritual. For example, many smokers will do the same thing each time, i.e. tap their pack, light up, and inhale deeply. They will then hold that breath for a moment or two, and let it out in a slow, steady stream.

In fact, this may be one of the principle reasons smokers say that smoking helps them deal with stress . . . it may be the only time in their life that they take a deep breath! Unfortunately, for us nonsmokers, it means we may never take a deep breath! We just go around breathing short and shallow breaths until we become really stressed and stop breathing altogether (which, by the way, has been proven to be very hazardous to one's health).

So, what can we learn from this example if our goal is to regain control, change the chemical makeup of our body, and shift our thinking to the top of the mind? First, the smokers are responding to a signal in such a way that a change in behavior (going to have a smoke) becomes more important than anything else. Remember when I said that stress can be seen not as the problem, but a valuable signal that something needs to change? Remember when I suggested that we become aware of when we first feel "pushed over the top," and begin that downward spiral? What if we were to raise our awareness of what stress feels like so that at the first sign of frustration, anxiety, resentment, etc. we could stop and focus all of our attention on regaining control?

Then we could do what the smokers do, i.e., take a deep breath! You see, whenever we are feeling out of control, there is always one thing that we can control, and that is our breathing. That's why if you have ever read a "stress management" book or attended a "stress management" seminar, you were probably told to "take a deep breath" when stressed.

The problem with this advice was the implication that this is all it takes to deal with the frustration, anger, and/or anxiety associated with a negative event, and we all know that just isn't true! In fact, if all we do is breathe deeply when stressed, we will just hyperventilate sooner or later because this doesn't solve the problem. Therefore, I am not going to suggest that this is where we should stop. However, I am going to suggest that this is where we should start, and here's why: Remember, when I labeled the three parts of the brain and described what function each part controlled?

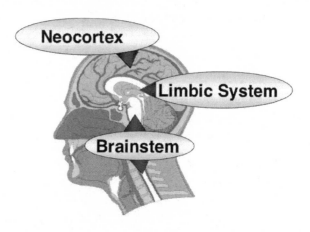

As mentioned earlier, the part that normally controls our breathing is the brainstem. However, when we decide to take a deep breath, the part of the brain that is making that decision is the neocortex! This means that the upper 80% of our brain (what I call the "Top of the Mind") where we have access to our problem-solving skills, interpersonal skills, creativity, knowledge, etc., has actually taken over a function normally controlled by the brainstem, and thus has literally regained control!

Now, in order for this to be effective, it must be done SLOWLY! I encourage you to use the 4-4-4 method where you inhale for a count of four, hold the breath for a count of four, and exhale for a count of four. This will ensure that you are breathing in such a way that it is being directed by the neocortex versus the brainstem.

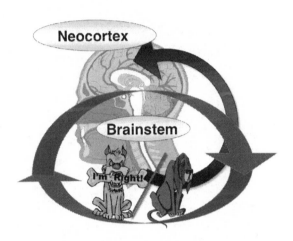

Another advantage of coming from the neocortex is that this upper 80% of the brain triggers the production of different chemicals. Rather than experiencing the effects of adrenaline and cortisol, you are now beginning to trigger the production of serotonin, dopamine, and endorphins, the chemicals that help us think clearer and feel better. That's the good news. The bad news is that this only deals with one aspect of the "cycle of stress," so let's move on to ensure that the system you are learning is compre-hensive in its ability to both deal with the problem, and sustain a solution.

CHAPTER 5

Dealing with Tension

The second characteristic of being stuck in the brainstem is *muscle tension*. This is due to the chemicals released when stressed (anxious, frustrated, worried, etc.), that are designed to get us ready to fight or flee. This tension is usually experienced as a tightness around the neck and shoulders, however, it can also manifest as tension all over the body and/or tension headaches.

In my seminars, I help participants understand the effect of this aspect of the problem by having them tense up all of the muscles in their body, and then trying to accomplish some task. What becomes clear is that regardless of the simplicity of the task (even if it is only mental), the tension will interfere with their ability to be successful. Plus, this exercise explains one of the reasons why so many people feel so exhausted today. Even though most of the effort we are putting fourth is mental versus physical, many people report feeling fatigued at some point in their day. This is because our brainstem is producing chemicals that tense our muscles, and we are constantly fighting this muscle tension as we go through our day.

Fortunately, there is a word that will deal very nicely with this tension, and that word is "relax." Unfortunately, there is a problem with this word. Have you ever gone up to someone who was clearly stressed and said, "Listen! If you would just calm down and relax...!" Would it be fair to say that they generally don't say, "Gee, never thought of that. Calm down, what a wonderful idea." No. The most common response to this suggestion is defensiveness.

"Calm down?!? Don't tell me to calm down!@#$%&*#@!!"

In other words, they will most likely start defending their right to be stressed! Why? Because in our culture, most people believe that if you aren't stressed, you must not care about what you are doing!

This is why when asked, "How are you doing?" most people will not respond with, "Happy and relaxed, thank you," even if this is true! In other words, even if they do feel happy and relaxed, they are reluctant to tell anyone out of fear that it will be misinterpreted as meaning they don't care, or that they are not taking their craft seriously. In fact, when asked, "How are you doing?" most people will start detailing how worried they are about the monologue, song, dance number, writing assignment, audition, test, etc., that is coming up. They do this for several reasons, but mostly to convince everyone that they do take their craft seriously.

Bottom line, because our culture sees "relaxing" as giving up or giving in (or at the very least what one can do only after one has checked off everything on their list), we see it as a problem instead of part of the solution. In fact, our culture has a name for people who relax before they have checked off everything on their list...we call them lazy slackers!

As you can see, there are several problems with the perspective that you have to be stressed to be seen as caring about your work: (A) Muscle tension is a natural, chemical response to a perceived threat and emanates from the brainstem. (B) Unless the situation calls for a fight-or-flight response, this muscle tension will only interfere with our ability to be successful, and even produce fatigue and exhaustion. (C) What is needed (relaxing to diminish the muscle tension) is seen as a character flaw. Therefore, to be successful, we must redefine the word, "relax," so that it becomes part of the solution and supports our neocortex ("Top of the Mind") in regaining control.

When I think of the word "relax," it reminds me not of giving up or giving in, but of another term I learned in childhood. I grew up in a small town in east Texas with older parents. In fact, my mother and father had been married twenty-five years before I was born, and I was their only child!. My mom went to the doctor when she was 45 years old and said, "Doc, I'm sick," and he replied, "No, you're pregnant," which, I'm sure brought about at least as much surprise (and maybe even stress) as it did joy.

Suffice it to say, I wasn't a planned child. However, there was a positive aspect in my being born so late in their lives. You see, my father was an alcoholic, and had been drinking for 22 years of their marriage. He stopped drinking three years before I was born, which means instead of being born and raised in the home of an active alcoholic, I was brought up in the home of a recovering alcoholic, and trust me, there is a huge difference.

The way my Dad stayed sober was through the program of Alcoholics Anonymous (AA) which means that we went to a LOT of AA meetings! In fact, we went to at least three to five AA meetings a week. However, rather than seeing this as strange or abnormal, I just thought this is what everyone did! As I grew up and learned how to read, I began examining the sayings posted on the walls of these gatherings, and, as you might imagine, there were quite a few ("One day at a time," "Let go and let God," etc.) that, even at a young age, I found meaningful. My favorite, however, was the "Serenity Prayer" which of course says, "God grant me the serenity to accept the things I cannot change, the courage to change the things I can, and the wisdom to know the difference."

This has become a very popular prayer. However, I wonder how many of us have ever looked closely at how it's put together, and what it's really saying. It's not the "get it all done" prayer or the "make everyone be the way I want" prayer. It isn't even a plea for serenity, or a promise that serenity will be the reward for accepting what we can't change and/or changing what we can. The Serenity Prayer is actually a formula for success!

For example, let's look at the first line: God grant me the serenity to (so that I might first) accept the things I cannot change. Think for a moment... how much of your stress, frustration, anxiety, etc., would be gone if you could accept what you cannot change? To what degree would this ability diminish the negative effects of auditions, deadlines, difficult people, etc., and support your success? For most of us, this ability to "accept" would make a significant difference in the amount of stress and/or frustration that we experience on a daily basis.

Now, just to be clear, I'm not one of those people who say: "You can't change the world, you can only change yourself." I believe in being as influential as possible in all aspects of our lives. I think we all can agree, however, that when we are frustrated, angry, frazzled, and stressed, our influence is diminished because, for one reason, people don't view overly emotional people as having high credibility. They tend to write them off as "out of control" or "not knowing what they are saying."

Plus, we now know that when we are feeling these negative emotions, we are trapped in the lower 20% of our brain and limited to either fight-or-flight. Basically, we don't have access to the sort of interpersonal skills, problem-solving skills, clarity, confidence, and creativity that allow us to impact the world around us.

This is where the concept of relaxing using the Serenity Prayer can help. For example, serenity and acceptance (the first two things that are asked for in the Serenity Prayer) allow us to do two things. First, serenity, being a neocortex perspective, ensures that we are coming from the top of our mind. From this upper 80%, we can make more purposeful decisions about how and where we focus our energy. Once we have accepted the things we can't change (which allows us to avoid wasting our energy on people and problems over which we have no control), we can set about "changing what we can," which we all know will often take courage. Put it all together and you get a formula for success.

We first create a moment of serenity which allows us to accept what we can't change. Then, because we are now coming from our neocortex, we can summon the courage to change the things we can, which for the moment is the chemical makeup of our body, and also which part of our brain is engaged in solving the problem. Once we have accomplished this, we will be in a much better position to bring this top of the mind perspective to the situation and see if there is indeed some way we can be influential.

Given that we have just made serenity a very important component in our ability to access the "top of our mind," let me ask you a question. On average, about how many minutes a day would you say you spend creating serenity in your life ? If you're like most of us, the answer would be zero! Most of us wake up in the morning to an alarm clock, and then commence pushing the snooze button repeatedly until we absolutely "have to" get out of bed. This means we are already late, and so we rush through the routine of getting ready. While doing this, we are often worrying about what problems our being late are going to cause. We then get in traffic, which we resent and fight in a vain attempt to make up for the time we overslept. When we finally get to our first class (or wherever) we are so frazzled that it is difficult to concentrate, much less create art.

When lunchtime comes, we may take thirty minutes for lunch, struggling to eat as much as we can in the smallest amount of time. Then, we are back doing whatever we consider most important, which is often what paper/project is due next!

At the end of the day when most students are going home to study, we have rehearsals, auditions, master classes, or some other extra work. Eventually, we do go home, collapse on the couch and begin scouring the internet looking for posts from friends or the latest viral video, thinking that, at last, we have found serenity. No! That's not serenity, that's exhaustion!

This is why serenity is the first thing that is asked for in the prayer. In order for us to succeed, *serenity* must be a precursor to acceptance, courage, wisdom, and change...not just what we get at the end of the day or after everything has been checked off of our list. In the same vein, the word "relax" isn't just an admonishment for being tense, but instead incorporates the concepts of serenity, acceptance, courage, wisdom, and change into one very powerful command.

Plus, when paired with the purposeful behavior of taking a series of deep breaths (i.e. saying the word "relax" on each exhale) this further establishes the neocortex as "who's in charge." Why? Because, both muscle tension and breathing are normally controlled by the brainstem. Therefore, when we inhale for a count of four, hold the breath for a count of four, and exhale slowly, saying the word "relax," we have the neocortex taking over two functions normally controlled by the brainstem.

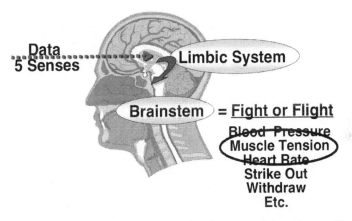

The key here is to do this combination of behaviors (breathing in deeply and saying the word "relax" on the exhale) in such a way and enough times to be effective. In other words, just inhaling quickly and barking "relax" when you exhale will not produce the effect you want. While small, our brainstem is very powerful, and is used to being in charge when perceived problems arise. Therefore, it will take a very concerted effort to go against what seems to be "natural" (i.e. running the problem over and over in our mind and justifying our anxiety, anger, and frustration) and choose serenity over righteous indignation, or the fear that we are some how "not enough."

If, however, you have determined that coming

from the top of your mind is important to you, taking three to five slow, deep breaths and saying the word "relax" on the exhale will deal very nicely with the first two physical aspects of stress and allow you to regain control.

That being said, accessing our best is more than just regaining control. Let's continue with this model and learn how to identify what we want to start (or, who we are at our best) as well as what we are trying to stop.

CHAPTER 6

The Psychological Aspects of a Top of the Mind Perspective

As mentioned, breathing and relaxing, while helpful, will not completely solve the problem, because in addition to the physical aspects of stress, there are very powerful psychological factors at work here as well. One of these is what has been called "mind chatter," negative self-talk, or what I call "brainstem questions."

For example, think of the last time you dealt with a stressful, and/or problematic situation. Do you remember the sort of questions that were running through your mind? Wasn't it something like, "What is wrong with me, why can't I get it together?" or "Why do I always hit the worst traffic?" or "Why am I not getting callbacks?" or "How rude, how could they talk about me that way?" or something similar?

While common, questions such as these are problematic because of the effect they have on our brain. For example, in certain ways, our brain works like a computer. If you ask a computer a question (i.e. type it in and hit "send" or "enter"), it will go searching its data banks for the answer. It doesn't stop to determine whether this is a good question or bad, helpful or not helpful. It simply attempts to answer the question that is asked. Plus, the answer must be in the particular database that is being searched in order for the computer to find it. In many ways, our brain is the same way.

For example, when we become stressed, frustrated, etc., and start asking questions, such as, "What's wrong with me?" or "Why am I not getting parts?" our brain thinks we want the answer! Further, because these questions are about the problem, our mind goes searching its brainstem data banks and probably comes up with responses like, "Well, you're just not good enough." Or "Your parents were right, you will never make a living at this." Of course, this doesn't help!

You see, we are using our computer-like mind to search the wrong database, or asking ourselves brainstem questions to which we really don't want the answer, or at best, questions that don't offer any solution. In fact, they produce chemical reactions that actually make the situation seem even worse and trap us in the lower 20% of our brain.

Given that what we want is to shift from the brainstem to the neocortex, I suggest that we continue to ensure that this upper part of our brain is in charge by asking "neocortex questions," or questions that shift our focus from the problem to the solution, and allow our brain to search the data located in the "top of our mind." In other words, we take three to five deep breaths saying the word "relax" on the exhale, and then we ask a question to which we do want the answer. One such question could be, "How would I rather be feeling?"

Interestingly enough, when I ask this question to participants in my seminars, the first response is often a blank stare. This is in stark contrast to their enthusiastic participation when asked to describe the problems in their lives and how these problems made them feel. However, when I ask the question, "How would you rather be feeling?" most people, at first, have no reply.

The reason behind this lack of response is simple. When we are focused on the problem and/or the pain of the problem, we are coming from the lower 20% of our brain, and thus cannot imagine (much less answer questions about) a solution. This is why there are two steps prior to asking, "How would I rather be feeling?" The deep breathing and saying the word "relax" on the exhale are designed to allow our neocortex to regain control so that we can begin asking questions about the solution versus continuing to fume about the problem.

Once I have given participants in my seminars time to shift to their neocortex, most eventually do come up with answers to the "How would I rather be feeling?" question. Interestingly enough, the first answers are often the antithesis of the problem. In other words, if they were originally stressed, they now want to feel calm or serene. While I certainly have no problem with people choosing to feel calm over feeling stressed, I want to be careful not to imply that this is the only choice. For example, rather than feeling calm, some people would like to feel confident, powerful, happy, or excited.

The good news is that in this model of change, you can choose any response you like, which means that you will not be forced to become calm when you would rather be excited, or serene when you want to feel confident and powerful. The important thing is that you allow the "top of your mind" to choose how you want to feel so that you have a neocortex-generated goal versus a brainstem-generated response.

CHAPTER 7

Dealing with Worry

Of course, as important as this third step is in the process of shifting from the brainstem to the neocortex, just asking ourselves about how we would rather be feeling doesn't accomplish this shift. The reason that this question is necessary but not sufficient to create change is due to the fact that when most of us are stressed, frustrated, etc., what we are actually doing is worrying about some problematic person or situation.

We are afraid that something either has gone wrong, is going wrong, or will go wrong, and are most likely spending much of our time running one or more of these problematic scenarios over and over in our mind. In fact, we may even see our worry as a necessary part of solving the problem, i.e., if we didn't worry, we wouldn't be thinking about the problem at all.

This tendency to see worry as a sign of caring, importance, or at the very least, a necessary aspect of successful problem-solving is a big factor in many people's lives. It's almost as if we judge the degree to which someone is involved or engaged in a situation by how worried they are about it. Lots of worry (stress, consternation, etc.) is interpreted to mean that a person is appropriately engaged in solving the problem, and/or is working at capacity, while little to no worry means that they don't care. Further, we tend to see people who aren't worried as unprepared. For example, when you meet someone who isn't worried, don't you get a little worried about them... almost as if it's dangerous not to be worried?

It's my belief that this mind-set originates in childhood. Just think... when you were a little kid and you were about to go out and play, what did your mom almost always say to you? Was "Be careful" one of her admonitions, and didn't this really mean "Watch out for bad things happening? Plus, didn't our parents tell us what we should be worried about? Playing in the street, men with candy, big dogs, etc. In other words, the message was that if we worried sufficiently about the bad things that could happen to us, somehow we would be safe from them, or put another way . . . worry keeps us safe.

Just to be clear, I am not suggesting that we shouldn't tell kids to be careful. However, if we look at the word "careful," what it really means is "full of care." My guess is that when as children we heard our mom say "Be careful," we did not interpret this to mean "be full of care for yourself and others." No, we heard this as "watch out (or beware of) bad things happening to you."

The problem, of course, is that unless we are in a true fight-or-flight situation, worry doesn't keep us safe, but rather it sends data to the lower 20% of our brain and limits our ability to respond. Further, all of this change in brain function and triggering of stress-related chemicals happens whether the situation we are worried about is happening at the moment or not!

In my seminars, I demonstrate this phenomenon by asking the participants to imagine holding a lemon. I suggest that they feel the weight of the lemon, and see the bumpy, yellow rind of the lemon in their hand. Next, I ask them to imagine cutting the lemon in half, feel the lemon juice running down their hand, see the shiny yellow pulp on the inside of the fruit, squeeze the lemon and watch the juice squirt out, and even begin to smell the lemon juice. Finally, I ask them to imagine actually taking a big bite out of their lemon, and feel the juice squirt out in their mouths!

As you might imagine, at this point most people are wrinkling up their faces, swallowing excess saliva, and basically reacting as if they had actually bitten into a real lemon! Of course, the lemon was only in their imagination. They knew that they weren't biting into a real lemon, but their brain and body reacted as if they were! In other words, the production of excess saliva and wrinkling of the facial muscles (which were actually reflective of chemical changes in their mouths) was a reaction to an imagined stimuli that they knew didn't exist! They had just changed the chemical makeup of their body, not by what they held in their hand, but what they held in their imagination!

How does this apply to dealing with our worries about life? Well, when we find ourselves worrying about something, how often is that particular situation actually happening at that particular moment? Is it fair to say not very often? This reminds me of a cartoon noticed on a tombstone on which was written the phrase, "Ninety percent of what killed me NEVER HAPPENED!!!!!!

What this demonstrates is that the body responds chemically to any image we hold in our mind, whether it is actually happening or not!

Of course, the problem here is that not only are we producing chemicals which throw our body into a heightened state of tension and stress, but also the fact that what we are worried about isn't actually happening (which means we can't do anything about it at the moment) and this only adds to the feeling of powerlessness and frustration.

In my seminars, I often bring up another example of the power of our mind to create chemicals in our body by asking the participants how many have ever had a sexual fantasy? Then, before anyone can answer, and while most are chuckling at the prospect, I point out that during the fantasy, they knew whatever they were imagining wasn't really happening ... but their body thought it was! Meaning that again, our body changes chemically to any image we hold in our mind.

How does all of this relate to "worry"? Well, when we are worrying, aren't we almost always creating an image of what we are worrying about? Don't we see the problematic person or situation very clearly and in great detail, and further, don't we spend a lot of energy running this image over and over in our mind? If so, now we know why this rarely helps us solve the problem, because, rather than helping us access the most creative and skilled parts of our brain, the problematic image is seen by the limbic system as a threat, which results in our brainstem being activated and our options limited to fight-or-flight.

Further, as we have discussed, the brainstem produces adrenaline, noradrenaline, and cortisol in response to this image, and thus elevates our heart rate, blood pressure, and muscle tension.

For those of you who are interested in how this reaction affects your health, here's how all of this works. When cortisol is released by the brainstem, it rushes throughout our body, shutting down our immune system (as well as other nonessential functions such as our digestive system), shutting down the production of protein, and increasing the production of glucose.

If we are not in a fight-or-flight situation where we either need the extra energy provided by the glucose, or are engaged in the sort of physical activity that would burn it off, it (the glucose) just sits in our system and turns into sugar. This is why if you have ever worried for any length of time, you might find yourself becoming nervous and fidgety, almost as if you have eaten too many candy bars.

It's also why many people have a hard time losing weight when they are stressed and upset for extended periods of time. They are constantly producing extra glucose/sugar from the ongoing production of cortisol, and this just turns into fat. (more information on this in Chapter 22)

Further, our immune system is based upon white blood cells, and the building block of white blood cells is protein. Therefore, when cortisol is constantly rushing throughout our body shutting down our production of protein, we have less protein available to build white blood cells, we have less white blood cells available to strengthen our immune system. . .AND WE GET SICK! Now, remember, this part of the book is about the negative effects of worry, so I don't want you to WORRY about this! I just want you to know that we have the power to influence the chemical makeup of our body by the images we hold in our mind. By the way, this also applies to the stories we tell about ourselves and others, which means we want to become more purposeful with respect to these images as well.

How can we use this phenomenon to our advantage? Well, we can see stress/frustration as a valuable signal and at the first sign of this reaction, we can have our neocortex regain control by taking three to five deep breaths using the word "relax" on the exhale. We can then further solidify our neocortex as the dominant part of our brain by asking "neocortex" questions, or questions to which we DO want the answer, as well as questions that lead us away from the problem and toward a solution, such as, "How would I rather be feeling?" Next, we can use the fact that our body will respond chemically to any image we hold in our mind to imagine feeling what we want to feel, or being how we want to be, versus worrying about the problem.

The most powerful way to practice this imagining is to first think of a time in your past when you were feeling how you want to feel now. For example, if you want to feel calm, just think of a time when you have felt calm in the past. The same applies to confident, in control, serene, or however you want to feel at the moment. Unfortunately, some people have difficulty with this step because they try to imagine a time when they felt calm, confident, in control, etc., in a situation that is similar to the one they see as the problem. In my seminars, it is common for participants to say, "Well, sure, I'd like to feel confident in auditions, BUT I'VE NEVER FELT CONFIDENT IN AUDITIONS, so I have nothing to draw from."

Fortunately, there is a simple answer to this dilemma. You see, it's not important, necessary, nor even expected that you will have a memory of feeling the way you want to feel in the current situation. All you have to do is remember a time in the past when you felt calm, confident, in control, or however you want to feel now. Remember, the body will respond chemically to any image we hold in our mind, so just remembering a time in the past when you felt how you want to feel now is a great first step.

It is important, however, for this image to be as vivid as possible. For example, remember how I described biting into the lemon in detail? I included many of our five senses in the description (feel the weight and texture of the lemon in your hand, see the shiny, yellow pulp, smell the pungent odor of the lemon, and finally taste the bitter juice by biting into the lemon). Similarly, you can use all of your five senses in remembering a time in the past when you were feeling how you want to feel now... where were you, what sounds did you hear, what was the temperature of the air, what aromas did you smell, if you reached out and touched anything in your image, what would it feel like (texture)? Bottom line, the more you engage all of your senses, and the more detail you employ in creating this image, the more successful you will be in effecting the chemical makeup of your body, which generally means producing endorphins versus adrenaline and cortisol.

This is not to say that you should just imagine yourself relaxing on a beach somewhere. Unlike other methods of dealing with problems and/or becoming more successful, "Life from the Top of the Mind" doesn't just try to give you a mental escape from the challenges of everyday life. Or, put another way, this isn't about helping you escape to your "happy place." This methodology is about how to bring a certain mindset to life, and by so doing, effect (a) the chemical makeup of your body, (b) the part of your brain that is engaged, and (c) ultimately, your ability to influence the quality of your life. Therefore, the idea is to create an image that is as close to real life as possible so that it isn't the setting that is creating the effect.

Once you have created this detailed multisensory image of the past (feeling the way you want to feel now), the next step is to bring the feelings of calm, confident, in control (or however you want to feel) into the present. Again, this is done with the most powerful part of your brain, as well as the part over which you have total control...your imagination. In other words, first you create a detailed image of a time in the past when you were feeling how you want to feel now.

For example, is it fair to say that you *have* felt confident in a past performance? In fact, weren't there times when you were totally lost in the moment and loving the experience of being on stage in front of an audience, and bringing a character to life? If so, you can ask yourself, "If I were able to bring these feelings into this present situation (an audition, for example), how would I change? That is, if I were able to bring this sense of being engaged, confident, and immersed in a performance to this audition, what would be different? How would I feel differently?

Of course, since this is all done in your mind, you have complete control of the images you create, and, thus, you can answer your own question and create an image of you being however you want to be in any situation (taking a test, performing in an audition, talking to others). Again, the more detailed and multisensory the image, the more it will effect the chemical makeup of your brain and body, so don't hold back.

Finally, since we will most likely be dealing with many of these scenarios (auditions, difficult people, school, parents, etc.) in the future, rather than worrying about them (which actually is practicing engaging the brainstem and feeling bad), we can ask ourselves how we would like to deal with these situations in the future. We then create a detailed multisensory image of how we would like to respond, and this act of imagination becomes almost as powerful as a behavioral rehearsal, which means that rather than spending our time applying our mind to worrying about the problem, we have trained it on a vision of the solution that we control.

Okay, let's put all of this together and see what we have accomplished so far:

1. We have identified that certain situations/types of people, etc., have, in the past, triggered certain emotional and behavioral reactions, such as stress, frustration, anxiety, etc., which make the original situation seem worse. This triggers another reaction, and the cycle of stress/frustration is born and fed.

2. We have also identified how this external cycle is replicated by an internal cycle. Our limbic system interprets data in such a way that it sends information down to the brainstem (bypassing our neocortex), which in turn releases chemicals that increase our heart rate, blood pressure, and muscle tension. This, of course, limits our ability to respond to either fight-or-flight. We then attempt to solve the problem, but because we are now tense, hyperactive, stressed, frustrated, anxious, and/or confused, we are less than effective, and thus become even more

frustrated, tense, etc. The limbic system interprets this increase in negative emotion and decreased effectiveness as more negative data, and thus sends it right back down to the brainstem. As a result of all of this, we become trapped in the lower 20% of our brain.

Trapped!

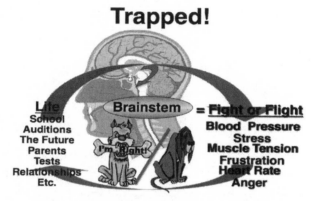

Life
School
Auditions
The Future
Parents
Tests
Relationships
Etc.

Brainstem = **Fight or Flight**
Blood Pressure
Stress
Muscle Tension
Frustration
Heart Rate
Anger

3. We have learned that in order to break this cycle and bring our best to life, we must change the chemical makeup of our body, and allow the "top of our mind" (our neocortex) to regain control.

4. One of the most effective ways of doing this is to have the neocortex take over one or more functions normally associated with our brainstem. Therefore, taking three to five deep breaths while saying the word "relax" on the exhale not only establishes the top of our mind as the most influential/dominant part of our brain, it also deals nicely with the muscle tension normally associated with stress.

5. Having accomplished this, we now can ask more

purposeful questions (such as, "How would I rather be feeling") which directs our neocortex to identify what we want (in terms of how we want to feel) versus focusing on the pain of the problem.

6. Finally, we can actually change how we feel by shifting from our brainstem to our neocortex and changing the chemical makeup of our body. We do this by utilizing the phenomenon that any image we hold in our mind produces a corresponding chemical change in our body, whether it is actually happening or not! Therefore, as we imagine a time in the past when we felt how we want to feel now, imagine bringing these feelings into the present, and then projecting this image/feeling into the future, we ensure that our neocortex is in control and producing serotonin, endorphins, and dopamine, rather than the adrenaline, noradrenaline, and cortisol associated with worry and/or frustration.

We are now ready to complete the first model by noticing or acknowledging the changes we have just produced (more calm, confident, in control, etc.). This is important because it allows us to take note of and appreciate what we have accomplished, which again is a neocortex activity.

One of the characteristics of an overly stressed, nonproductive mindset is that there is often little attention paid to achievements. Many hours are spent worrying about how problems from the past will negatively effect the future (which we now know only enhances the potential of this happening), but little if any thought is given to what has gone, or is going well. The fact that we have just allowed the top of our mind to regain control, relaxed our muscles so that we aren't fighting ourselves, shifted our thinking from the problem to the solution, and changed the chemical makeup of our body is quite remarkable. In order to take full advantage of these efforts, we must now notice these changes and give ourselves credit for the transformation. Plus, this last step, "Notice the change" makes the model spell BRAIN (Breathe, Relax, Ask, Imagine, Notice the change).

When I create models, I almost always try to make them spell something for several reasons. One, it makes the model, in this case, the BRAIN model, easier to remember and practice. Two, we are talking about changing how our "BRAIN" processes information, and signals other parts of our body to produce chemicals, and therefore, the spelling supports the goal.

Of course, every model comes with questions and concerns, and this one is no exception. One of the concerns that participants voice is their fear that working through the model will take too long. They think they don't have time to breathe, relax, ask how they would rather be feeling, imagine feeling this way in the past, present, and future, and then notice the changes. In fact, after hearing me present this model, I'm sure some people are thinking, "I don't have time to do this! If I had time to go through this model, I WOULDN'T BE STRESSED IN THE FIRST PLACE!!#%&*@%!!

While I can certainly understand this concern, I think we may want to look a little deeper at this resistance if living life from the "top of the mind" is truly our goal. For example, I suggest that the reason we think we don't have time to go through a model such as this is that we are not making our peace of mind and/or our ability to deal with stress/life a priority, and I believe that this is a mistake. In fact, I think our peace of mind/ability to come from the most productive part of our brain should be important... at least as important as, well... diarrhea!

Yes... diarrhea! Well, just think, when you have diarrhea, it becomes pretty important, doesn't it? Don't we stop everything we are doing to take care of it? We stop driving on the freeway, talking on the phone, everything! Notice, when people have diarrhea, they never say, "I don't have time to deal with this now," or "I'll just deal with this later." Plus, our culture even supports the importance of diarrhea in our lives. For example, when you are talking with someone and say something like, "Excuse me, but I have to run to the bathroom!" have you noticed that no one ever says, "Oh no, you stay right here!" No! Diarrhea has such universal importance that it is acknowledged as an excuse to stop anything! In fact, it's in the building code! You can't build a building without so many little rooms that if people have diarrhea, they can go there! How many "peace of mind" rooms do you see?

That's why I suggest that we make our peace of mind, and our ability to access the most productive, intelligent part of our brain and bring our best to life at least as important as diarrhea. If we would stop whatever we are doing for diarrhea, we should be willing to stop when we find ourselves trapped in the brainstem as well. This is where the phrase, "Stress is a signal that something needs to change" comes from, as well as the concept that "stress isn't the problem, but a very important part of the solution." Just as most of us respond very purposefully to the signal of diarrhea, we can begin to use stress as a valuable signal as well.

For example, when we first begin noticing the signals of stress (frustration, tension, anxiety, etc.), we can stop, excuse ourselves, and go to the restroom (or any other locale that offers us the opportunity to take a few minutes to regain control.) We can then begin to access our neocortex by taking three to five deep breaths, and saying the word "relax" on the exhale. Next, we can begin to ask more purposeful questions that have our brain searching the data in the "top of our mind" versus our brainstem for the solution (such as "How would I rather be feeling?") Further, because any image we hold in our mind creates a corresponding chemical reaction in our body, we can then use the most powerful part of our mind (our imagination) to change the chemical makeup of our brain and body by imagining feeling this way in the past, present, and future. Finally, after noticing or acknowledging how we are now more calm, confident, and in control, we can go back into the situation knowing that we have shifted from our brainstem to our neocortex, and are now responding from the top of our mind.

So, now I have given you a process (the BRAIN Model) for changing the chemical makeup of your body and shifting from your brainstem up into the top of your mind. As you might imagine, many people are excited to learn that stress is really just data being sent to the wrong part of our brain, which means it's not only something they can control, but that it can even be used as a valuable signal. The only problem with this process is that it is new, and thus has yet to become a habit. Therefore, if you would like to become skilled at influencing the chemical makeup of your body and how your brain processes information, then I encourage you to look for opportunities to practice this powerful model.

In fact, I encourage you to put this model to the test by using it in as many negative situations as possible. This should give you very good information as to how this behavioral model supports your ability to regain control and establish the upper 80% of your brain as the dominant influence of your thoughts and emotions.

Of course, most people want more. They not only want to know how to change or shift when stressed, they are interested in information that allows them to sustain this "Top of the Mind" perspective so that they don't keep falling back into the brainstem and the cycle of stress over and over again. That's coming up in Part Two.

Part II

CHAPTER 8

What <u>Doesn't</u> Change

The first part of this book has been about what to change and how to change. When feeling frustrated, stressed, anxious, confused, etc., you now know how to use these feelings as valuable signals that a change is needed. You have become more aware of what is happening chemically in your body and brain, and how to use the BRAIN model to change. The second part of this book is about how to maintain this new "top of the mind" perspective, regardless of the situation, or, put another way, how to live life based upon what *doesn't* change.

"There's a thread you follow.
It goes among things that change,
but <u>it doesn't change</u>.
People wonder about what you are
pursuing.
You have to explain about the thread,
but it is harder for others to see.
<u>*While you hold it, you can't get lost.*</u>
Tragedies happen, people get hurt
or die, and you grow old and die.
Nothing you do can stop time's
unfolding.
<u>*You don't ever let go of the thread!"*</u>

William Stafford

As you might imagine, this can be a much more involved process, and thus, I will introduce several models to support you in this new way of life. However, because so many people have told me that they find the BRAIN model to be tremendously valuable, I have also woven this behavioral process

into this new material with the goal of tying everything together and helping you succeed in living life
from the "Top of the Mind."

In order to accomplish this goal of sustaining
a "Top of the Mind" perspective, we must first have
a good idea of what this new way of being looks like.
I call it "**C³**" which stands for _Clarity, Confidence,_
and _Creativity._ I use these words not only because
they represent universal aspects of success which
emanate from our neocortex, but also because as we
examine the problem in terms of the cycle of stress/
frustration, we can see that there is very little clarity,
confidence, and creativity contained in the cycle.

In some ways, we have been using the model
from the beginning of this book. If you remember,
we began with a quote from Albert Einstein that
said "Problems cannot be solved at the same level
of awareness that created them." In other words,
trying to solve our problems by just becoming less
stressed, or worse, trying to change the negative
aspects of life so that we are no longer anxious will
never work. Instead, we must raise our awareness
about what is really happening to cause the problem

before we can break the cycle of stress and sustain true success.

Basically, this is what we did in Part One. We became clear about what really creates and sustains this cycle (the way our brain works and the chemicals it produces), and we learned how to shift to the more productive part of our brain and change the chemical makeup of our body.

However, in order to move beyond simply breaking the cycle to the point where we can actually access our confidence and creativity on a regular basis, we must become clear about other things as well. Therefore, I am going to continue to frame the material in Part Two in terms of "clarity," and demonstrate how an increase in awareness leads to a similar increase in confidence and creativity.

CHAPTER 9

Clarity About the Power of Purpose

The first step in the process is becoming clear about our purpose. I say this because I don't believe that when we are caught in the cycle of stress that we are responding to the negative aspects of life "on purpose." In other words, few, if any of us are deliberately becoming frustrated, stressed, anxious, or confused when faced with challenges such as tests, auditions, or difficult people, etc.

That doesn't mean we don't have a purpose. In fact, for many young artists, their purpose is "to be chosen." Whether this is being chosen by a school, for a callback, a part, or just being seen as "special" by the right people, this desire is at the root of a tremendous amount of stress. While this is understandable, given that our being chosen is beyond our control, this desire often manifests as fear of not being chosen and all the problems that could result.

Or, you may have heard some describe their purpose as survival. "If I can just get through the test, semester, audition, etc." Again, this is understandable, however, survival is also a brainstem function, and therefore can easily throw us into this lower 20% of the brain.

Instead, acording to Albert Einstein, ("Problems cannot be solved at the same level of awareness that created them."), what we need here is more awareness or clarity... clarity about what is most important *and is within our control*! In other words, I'm not saying that doing well in auditions, on tests, etc. isn't important. I'm just saying that these aspects of life can't be the "most important" because they are beyond your control. And...

You never want to make the most important thing in your life something that is beyond your control!

...because doing so is a recipe for stress and frustration.

Therefore, what we need is a way of thinking, feeling and being that:

1. Allows us to access the clear, confident, and creative part of the brain.

2. Allows us to get things done and deal with the challenging situations we encouter more successfully .

3. And... is within our control!

I call this way of being our "Highest Purpose" because it allows us to access the highest part of the brain, and when we make it the most important thing in our life, allows us to deal with everything else more sucessfully.

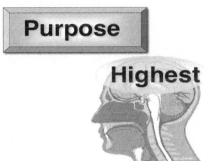

Unfortunately, this concept, while vital, can be somewhat ambiguous. Therefore, I have found a quote that helps clarify what is meant by "Highest Purpose" and makes it more concrete. It says:

"Every thought, emotion,
and action is a statement
about who we are,
and who we are becoming."
"So, why not make this statement
on purpose?"

As I have said earlier, I don't believe that we have been responding to the challenging aspects in our lives "on purpose" or deliberately. Nor do I believe that our old, negative reactions are purposeful statements about who we are. In other words, I don't think we have been purposefully defining ourselves as someone who is anxious, frustrated, stressed, resentful, etc. However, whenever we say that auditions make us nervous, or difficult people make us angry, what we are *really* saying is these situations have *the power to define us... or control us!*

If we don't want these situations to have this sort of power in our lives, we must take on that power ourselves. Of course, in order to define ourselves on purpose, we must have some idea of who we want to be, or the statement we want to make about who we are, and then make becoming this person our highest purpose... ALL THE TIME! Not just when we are "on," but in every aspect of our lives.

One way to do this is to put the statement in the form of a question (remember how powerful questions are?), and make sure it is a neocortex question, or a question that can only be answered by the upper 80% of the brain. One such question could be:

"If I were defining myself versus being defined by the difficult people and situations in my life, what are the qualities and characteristics I would like to be able to draw upon?"

Or,

"When dealing with difficult people, or challenging situations, I would like to be more_____?"

When I pose these questions to participants in my seminars, they come up with excellent responses. They say things like, calm, confident, understanding, knowledgeable, loving, flexible, rational, empathetic, creative, kind, helpful, powerful, relaxed, in control... all great answers, to be sure. However, it's not so important what other people think, the question is, what do you think... what would your list look like?

Having a sense of how you want to define yourself, or the qualities and characteristics you want to access in the future is a critical step in your success. Therefore, I suggest you stop reading for a moment and make your list. It can be pretty much anything you want, just make sure it is framed in terms of what you want versus what you don't want.

Not About "Nots"

I say this because many people initially try to create a solution by merely lessening the problem. In other words, when describing how they want to change, many people will say that they want to be less stressed, less frustrated, anxious, angry, etc. This is understandable, however, we now know that holding an image in our mind of what we *don't* want doesn't create what we *do* want. In fact, chances are that this image will actually trigger a chemical reaction similar to that of worry, which only throws our thinking into the lower part of our brain, and often has us producing what we are afraid of (becoming worried about worry or stressed about stress, etc.).

An example of this phenomenon is the experience of a small child, say around one and a half to two years old, who spills his milk. Often, because this creates a mess for the parent to clean up, it's not uncommon for the parent to become upset and admonish the child with something like, *"How many times have I told you to be careful with your milk!?! I am going to give you some more, but you better not spill it this time!"*

The child, of course is now worried about spilling the milk, and thoughts such as, *"Don't spill the milk... Don't spill the milk"* are likely to be going through his mind. The parent puts a new glass of milk in front of the child, and again tells him what he shouldn't do. *"Okay, now, here is a new glass of milk, you'd better not spill it this time!"* This, of course, only has the child worrying even more about spilling the milk, which makes the internal dialogue of, *"Don't spill the milk, Don't spill the milk!"* even louder and more desperate. It's not hard to predict what happens next. At some point, the child spills the milk. Why? Because the image that is running through his mind is what he is trying to avoid... spilling the milk!

You see, the mind does not register the word "not" with respect to the images it produces. For example, if I were to say to someone: "Do NOT think of a red elephant sitting in front of you," the image that would automatically spring to mind would be a red elephant. If you happen to be deathly afraid of red elephants, this would produce a brainstem reaction and a surge of fight-or-flight chemicals, such as adrenaline and cortisol. This is why phobias can be so debilitating. People very understandably try to avoid what frightens them, which only guarantees that they will think about it and be thrown into the brainstem as a result. Again, this has us producing what we fear, such as the child spilling his milk.

Therefore, when making your list, rather than less stressed, you want to choose something like calm or relaxed, rather than less judgemental, you might choose tolerant, etc.

Bottom line, this book is not about "nots." Or, as my friend, Mike Darley, once said,

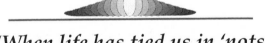

"When life has tied us in 'nots,' courage, hope, and optimism can be our undoing."
Mike Darley

There is also another quote that came to me

during a session that seems to sum up this philosophy of shifting from avoiding the problem to creating a more purposeful solution. It says:

"When our purpose becomes avoidance, our life becomes a void."

This means that we can't make simply avoiding certain people or situations our highest purpose if we want to create a life of meaning and fulfillment, because the energy of avoidance is based upon what we don't want. All it will produce is a void (which is fueled and filled with fear).

Okay, let's make your first draft of your list now. You might want to include the energies of both Yin and Yang in your list so that there is a combination of gentle and powerful. For example, calm and confident, understanding and knowledgeable, loving and flexible, rational and empathetic. etc. Again, here are the questions that should be helpful:

"If I were dealing with life in a way that made a statement about who I am, what are the qualities and characteristics I would like to be able to draw upon?" - Or...
"When dealing with difficult people, or challenging situations, I would like to be

more_____?"

Feel free to put them in the margins of this book or on a separate piece of paper. Where you write them isn't important. What is important is your taking a moment to determine what you want to think and feel in the future. I can't help you get to where you want to go if you haven't determined what that destination looks like.

Now that you have your list, notice how it differs from the list of old reactions. Can you see how anxious, stressed, frustrated, angry, resentful, etc. all come from the lower 20% of the brain, while your new list of more purposeful responses come from the upper 80% of the brain, or the "Top of the Mind?" If so, you now get to decide how important this is to you. In other words, how valuable would it be if instead of reacting to the triggers with the brainstem...

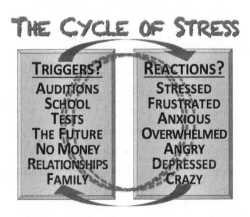

THE CYCLE OF STRESS

TRIGGERS?	REACTIONS?
AUDITIONS	STRESSED
SCHOOL	FRUSTRATED
TESTS	ANXIOUS
THE FUTURE	OVERWHELMED
NO MONEY	ANGRY
RELATIONSHIPS	DEPRESSED
FAMILY	CRAZY

... you could respond with something like this?

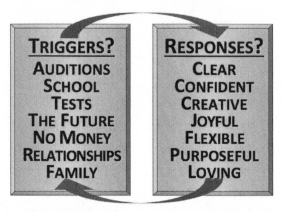

TRIGGERS?	RESPONSES?
AUDITIONS	CLEAR
SCHOOL	CONFIDENT
TESTS	CREATIVE
THE FUTURE	JOYFUL
NO MONEY	FLEXIBLE
RELATIONSHIPS	PURPOSEFUL
FAMILY	LOVING

Of course, you might have a very different list. What is important is that you have a vision of who you want to be, and are willing to make defining who you are your "Highest Purpose" (the most important thing in your life). In addition, it's important that you see life not as what is being done to you, but an opportunity to practice defining yourself in a way you would recommend to someone you love.

You see, I believe that we are always practicing something, and life will always give us plenty of opportunities to practice. This means that we will either be practicing the new, more purposeful ways of being, or the old, habitual reactions.

One good example of using life as a place to practice comes from a colleague of mine. He told me about a student who came to him complaining about a classmate who was "driving him crazy." The student was convinced that this classmate was the source of 90% of his misery, and if he could just learn to deal with this person, he would be a happy guy. My colleague immediately agreed to help, and began to describe what needed to be done.

"First," he said, *"we will go to the local acting studio and spend some time auditioning actors that look and sound like the person that is bothering you. Next, you will need to write this actor a script, which shouldn't be very difficult because I'm sure you know exactly how he talks and the sort of things he says that bugs you. Then, we will spend approximately six weeks or so practicing with this actor. We will have him come to my office on a weekly basis and, in time, you will learn how to deal with people such as this so that they never again have the power to drive you crazy.*

Of course, you will have to pay the actor for his time, and unfortunately hiring an actor for six weeks of work will not be cheap . . . or . . . we could do this in a different way. You could practice with the actual, difficult person in your life FOR FREE! I would be working with you, of course, but because you are dealing with this person all the time (and thus getting in a lot of practice), the process won't take nearly as long. In fact, after you have become successful, you will now know how to deal with any similar person for the rest of your life!"

Another example of using the situations we deal with every day to practice responding "on purpose," actually happened to me. It began as an invitation to play golf. I am an avid (some might say rabid) fan of the game, and have even created a presentation on its mental and emotional aspects entitled, "Golf from the Top of the Mind."

At some point, I thought it would be a great idea to create a golf excursion where the participants would be able to hear a presentation on how the BRAIN model helps us shift to the neocortex, release muscle tension, and create the sort of mindset that allows us to play our best game. I set everything up at the Banff Springs Hotel in Banff, Canada, and sent out an announcement to those on my mailing list about the trip, and how to sign up.

One of the most interesting responses came from a good friend, and went something like this: *"In reference to your excursion to Banff, I think golf is a white man's elitist's game, and I will have nothing to do with it!"*

As you might imagine, I was at first somewhat taken aback by this response. However, if there is one thing I have learned, it's that if you put yourself up as a teacher of dealing with life, then you better be able to walk the talk. So, summoning my best thoughts, I responded in this way: *Dear Joe* (not his real name), *Given that I support people in following their beliefs and doing what they feel is right, I support your decision to not participate in the Banff experience."* To which (somewhat tongue in cheek) he replied : *"Hey, when I am trying to be angry with you and you respond in a nice way, it really pisses me off!"* To which I simply responded: *"Thanks for the opportunity to practice."*

The purpose of these stories is to give you at least two examples of what it means to use life (especially the negative aspects of life) versus life using us. When we decide that choosing how we want to define ourselves with respect to a particular situation is our goal, then we can begin to use those situations as opportunities to practice. The reason this is so powerful is that the process of defining ourselves on purpose, comes from the upper 80% of the brain, or the "Top of the Mind." In doing so, we are not only thinking differently, we are triggering the production of serotonin, endorphins, and dopamine, (the chemicals that help us think clearly and feel better) versus adrenaline, noradrenaline, and cortisol.

In other words, do you think that you will ever find yourself dealing with negative people and/ or difficult situations in the future? If the answer to this question is, "yes, of course," how valuable would it be for you to be *in* these situations, but not *of* them. . . to be able to interact with all types of people and/or difficult situations, and yet remain clear, confident, and creative? If this would be an achievement worth your time and effort, then the first step is to imagine that these situations exist as opportunities for you to practice, as if the scenario is a scene in a play, and your purpose is to step on stage and define your character.

Let me give you one final illustration to make

this step as clear as possible. Let's assume that there is a new television show called, "Life from the Top of the Mind." Twenty participants are chosen from all parts of the country and from all walks of life, and each is taken to a location that is made up of two distinct locales, and are told that this is where they will live for the next six months.

The first location is a resort-like atmosphere where the participant is pampered in luxury. They wake up each morning to breakfast in bed if they like, swimming under the palm trees, etc., followed by an hour or two spent with someone who is there to help them define their highest purpose, or the statement they want to make about who they are in "real life." Then, in the afternoon, each participant is taken to an environment that looks exactly like where they live. The classrooms and theaters look the same, and even the people they come in contact with in this "artificial" environment look and act exactly like the people they see every day.

The participants are told that their goal is to go into this environment and "practice" responding to the challenging people and situations they encounter in a way that is congruent with their highest purpose, or the qualities and characteristics they have identified. Their "practice time" is short at first, so that the participants only have to keep their focus for around five minutes. Let's assume that you are one of those participants. Don't you think you could practice responding in a purposeful manner even in the most difficult of situations for five minutes? The next day, the practice time is lengthened to 10 minutes, then to 20 and so on, until by the end of the six month period, the participant is spending almost the entire day practicing responding on purpose.

Can you see how, after six months of practicing responding in this purposeful way, you will likely become very good at this way of life? Further, can you see how after this extended period of practice, you would be able to return to your life and continue to respond in this more purposeful manner?

Of course, there is good news and bad news. The bad news is that we don't have a network or production company to create an environment in which we can practice, and the good news is that we don't need one. We already have it available to us . . . it's called life! You see, life will always give us plenty of opportunities to practice. We will either practice responding in the old ways we have identified (the cycle of stress) . . . or we will practice responding in the new ways we have identified as congruent with our highest purpose.

To support you in this process of clarifying what you want and/or who you want to be, I have come up with four neocortex questions which you can use in any situation to support you in bringing this "Top of the Mind" perspective to life. I call these questions "The Four Criteria" because you can use them as a criteria for deciding whether you want to hang on to an old reaction, or choose a new response. For example, let's first apply them to our old reactions, and then I will show you how to use them to shift to the upper 80% of the brain and increase your clarity, confidence, and creativity.

The Four Criteria:

1. Has this thought, emotion, or action been chosen deliberately, or on purpose? Most people say that they don't choose to be stressed or anxious on purpose. It just seems to happen to them.

2. How is it working for me? Meaning, to what degree is my stress, frustration, resentment, anxiety, etc., helping me become more effective in creating the life I want? Again, most people would not identify these reactions as highly effective or desirable.

3. Is this thought, emotion, or action making the statement I want to make about who I am? Just as most people say that they are not becoming stressed, annoyed, and/or frustrated on purpose, most would also say that these words would not be what they would choose to define who they are ("I am someone who is, frustrated, stressed, annoyed, etc.")

The first three questions of "The Four Criteria" can go a long way toward making this determination because, as discussed, they are "neocortex questions," and thus engage the upper 80% of our brain in the process of evaluation. However, the fourth question is one that many students report being the most powerful of all. It asks;:

4. Would I teach or recommend this thought, emotion, or action to someone I love?

When I get to this point in my master classes and ask this question, a knowing silence always falls over the participants, because few, if any of us, would purposefully teach someone we love to be stressed, frustrated, depressed, or anxious.

Thus, this question completes the initial evaluation of our thoughts and emotions in a very powerful way. Meaning, when looking at the cycle of stress...

we can say with confidence that, no I'm not feeling / thinking this way on purpose, it's not working for me, it's certainly not making the statement I want to make about who I am, **AND NO!** *I would never teach or recommend this way of being to someone I love!*

Having become clear about the old reactions, we are now in the position to use the Four Criteria to come up with a solution, meaning that we can now ask: "Okay, if I was choosing my thoughts, emotions, and actions on purpose...in a way that I believe would be most effective...in a way that makes the statement I want to make about who I am...and in a way I would teach/recommend to someone I love,"... what would that look like? How would I be thinking, feeling, and acting differently if this were the case?

Is it fair to say that your new way of responding to life might look something like this?

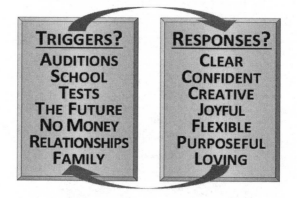

TRIGGERS?	RESPONSES?
AUDITIONS	CLEAR
SCHOOL	CONFIDENT
TESTS	CREATIVE
THE FUTURE	JOYFUL
NO MONEY	FLEXIBLE
RELATIONSHIPS	PURPOSEFUL
FAMILY	LOVING

Again, your list might be different, however, can you see how what you wrote down might fit The Four Criteria? And, can you also see how these more purposeful responses would be coming from the upper 80% of the brain and could be applied to almost any situation?

If so, it's also important to recognize that what we are doing here isn't stopping the less desirable reactions, but instead, starting the new, more purposeful ways of being. Or, put another way:

Creating the life we want isn't about what we are stopping... It's about what we are starting!

Because, when we are trying to stop an old way of being, we are almost always thinking about (worried about) what will happen if we don't stop it.

This has us becoming worried and anxious about our worry and anxiety. While this is understandable, it is ineffective, meaning we can't deal with worry and fear with worry and fear. It's like pulling up to a burning building with a flame thrower... it only makes the situation worse.

It's not that our stress and anxiety has no purpose. Remember, "Stress is a signal that something needs to change." We just can't use the energy of stress and anxiety to make the change, because stress and anxiety trigger the lower 20% of the brain, and trying to make purposeful change from this limited, reactive part of the brain doesn't work.

In other words, we can certainly use the problems caused by fear, drugs, alcohol, apathy, depression, eating disorders, etc. as good information about what needs to change. *We just can't use the negative energy triggered by these problems to make positive change!*

Instead, we must shift to the upper 80% of the brain (specifically the frontal lobes that allow us to move into the future in more purposeful ways) in order to make and sustain the changes we would recommend to someone we love.

The first step in this process is knowing what we want to change to, or the qualities and characteristics we want to access. In other words, your list. Therefore, this can be a good time to look at your list once again and make sure it meets the Four Criteria:
1. Your qualities and characteristics have been chosen on purpose.
2. You can see how they would be more effective than the old stress-related reactions.
3. They make the statement you want to make about who you are.

4. They represent what you would teach or recommend to someone you love.

In fact, the most effective way to lay out your new awareness is using the format below.

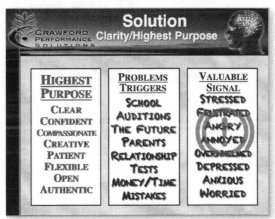

Here we have the triggers we identified as problematic, the old reactions (now described as a valuable signal about what part of the brain we are coming from), and our Highest Purpose, or the qualities and characteristics we choose to define who we are and that we would teach to someone we love. And further, this information is laid out in a way that can change an old reaction to a more purposeful way of being. For example:

When we are clear about the qualities and characteristics we want to access before we go into a situation, we can turn the problem into the practice field.

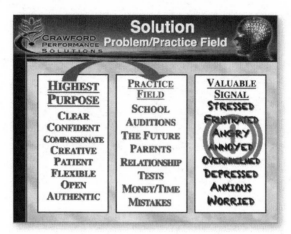

HIGHEST PURPOSE	PRACTICE FIELD	VALUABLE SIGNAL
CLEAR	SCHOOL	STRESSED
CONFIDENT	AUDITIONS	FRUSTRATED
COMPASSIONATE	THE FUTURE	ANGRY
CREATIVE	PARENTS	ANNOYED
PATIENT	RELATIONSHIP	OVERWHELMED
FLEXIBLE	TESTS	DEPRESSED
OPEN	MONEY/TIME	ANXIOUS
AUTHENTIC	MISTAKES	WORRIED

In other words, just as sports teams have a place to practice their offense and defense, and an artist has a place to rehearse or practice his or her lines or music, we can use life as a place to practice accessing the "Top of the Mind," and bringing our best to life.

Because we know what this looks like (who we are when we are confident, creative, flexible, compassionate, etc.) we will be going into the situation (a test, an audition, a conversation, etc.) already in the upper 80% of our brain, and triggering the production of success-related chemicals such as serotonin and endorphins.

Plus, we will be making our "Highest Purpose," or the most important thing we will do in the situation, our willingness to access these qualities. And, because this is within our control (we are not needing someone or something to change in order to be this way), the potential that we will be successful is very high. In fact, it is very possible that we will not only be successful in continuing to be a way we would recommend to someone we love, but also that we will be dealing with the situation more successfully, because when we are coming from the "Top of the Mind," we are also bringing our best interpersonal skills, problem-solving skills, performing skills, etc. to the experience.

The key, however, is that we must make this our Highest Purpose, or the most important thing we are doing!

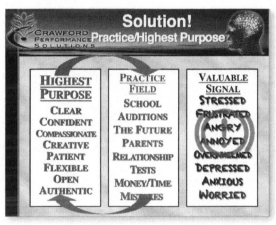

If we allow something else to become more important (getting the part, moving the audience, doing it right, etc.) the old fears around what will happen if we don't (get the part, move the audience, get it right, etc), will throw us into the brainstem.

All of these things are important, to be sure. They just can't be the *most* important because they are either not within our control, or they require us to be perfect. This new way of being is not about being perfect, just purposeful, which means we can use both our successes and "failures," or those times when we are not able to stay in the "Top of the Mind" as good information about what works and what we want to practice more purposefully next time.

For those of you who liked the BRAIN model in the first half of the book, you can use it here as well. For example, you can take three to five deep breaths saying the word "relax" on the exhale, which establishes the neocortex as the dominant part of your brain. Then, you could change the neocortex question in the "Ask" step of the model from, "How would I rather be feeling?" to The Four Criteria:

1. Am I choosing how I want to feel, think, and act, on purpose or deliberately?

2. Is it working for me, or helping me create the experience of life I want?

3. Does my way of being make the statement I want to make about who I am?

4. Would I teach, or recommend this thought, emotion, or action to someone I love?

When we are being less than purposeful, the answer to these questions will almost always be "no." Then, as mentioned earlier, we can turn the questions around to raise our awareness of how we do want to be.

"Okay, if I was choosing my thoughts, emotions, and actions on purpose...in a way that I believe would be most effective...in a way that makes the statement I want to make about who I am...and in a way I would teach/recommend to someone I love,"... what would that look like? How would I be thinking, feeling, and acting differently if this were the case?

Of course, while extremely valuable, the idea of identifying who you want to be, and seeing life as an opportunity to practice implementing this self-definition is only the first step of a more inclusive, five-step model. Let's continue to the second step to understand one of the true causes of how we think, feel, and act, and how you can become more influential in this process.

CHAPTER 10

Clarity About Our Past

I f you remember, the second part of this book is based upon the C³ Model of Clarity, Confidence, and Creativity, and we began by becoming clear about the importance of dealing with the negative aspects of life "on purpose." Now we must become clear about why we find ourselves stuck in the Cycle of Frustration & Stress in the first place, and how we can use this knowledge to align our thoughts, emotions, and behavior with who we want to be. In other words, we must become clear about the true cause of why we think, feel, and act in certain ways, and what we can do to become more influential in this process.

From my perspective, there are two principle causes, and the first is "our past." When I refer to our past, I mean any old habits, tendencies, beliefs, and / or learned perspectives that may be incongruent with our highest purpose. Let's face it. Our past is where we learned who we were, or were expected to be. Our past is also where we learned how to react to situations and other people in general. Basically, our past is where we learned what the world was like, and our place in this world.

It didn't matter that "the world" we saw was mostly what went on in our family. In fact, most of us didn't think, "This is just how my family is." We just thought, "This is how the world is," and from this experience, we formed our core beliefs, habitual ways of reacting to the world, preconceptions of life, etc. And, in many ways, we continue to repeat these habitual ways of being today. This shouldn't be surprising. The reason they call them habits is because they're habitual, which means we seem to find ourselves behaving and reacting without our conscious thought.

Don't get me wrong. I'm not saying that everything, or even most of what we learned from our past is bad or wrong, or even incongruent with our purpose. I'm sure that some of what you learned serves you very well today, and that you may want to hold on to this aspect of your past. The good news is that you will (hold onto what you learned, that is). The reason I can say this with such certainty is because this learning has taken the form of a habit or core belief. This doesn't mean that we can't change our core beliefs if we find they are incongruent with our purpose. It just means that we may want to hold on to some of our learning, and, if this is the case, we needn't do a thing because it is woven into the fabric of who we have become.

For example, I remember something that I learned from my past that is very congruent with, or supportive of, my purpose today. If you remember, I described my past as growing up in the home of a recovering alcoholic. Both my mom and dad were very active in the programs of Alcoholics Anonymous and Al Anon, and, from as early as I can remember, our lives revolved around going to meetings and interacting with other people and families in the program.

Our kitchen table was a place that people would come on a regular basis to pour their hearts out and, often, turn their lives around. Dad was always talking to someone on the phone, going out in the middle of the night on "twelve-step calls," and attending AA meetings. In fact, as I mentioned earlier, we went to meetings so often it was almost like going to McDonald's to me, because I remember playing around the meeting halls and watching my mom and dad stand up in front of all those people and tell their story, over and over again.

Consequently, I have never had a fear of public speaking. In my studies, I have learned that this is one of the most common of all our fears, more so than snakes, or heights, or even death! However, because I saw my parents speak at AA meetings on a regular basis, it never even occurred to me that speaking to large groups of people was something to be afraid of. In fact, I have a tape of myself at the age of five speaking at an AA meeting, and while I can't make out what I was saying, I was clearly saying it with confidence because I had watched my mom and dad do this so often.

Given that this has been such a natural part of my growing up and learning about the world, to this day, I have never imagined that speaking in front of a group of five hundred or five thousand was anything to be frightened of. In other words, this part of my past, or the legacy that was given to me by my mother and father, is very congruent with my purpose. I didn't learn it "on purpose," however it serves me very well today. In fact, as a speaker, trainer, and counselor, this experience of growing up in this type of environment has given me a model for communicating and helping that has served me well, and continues to be a resource for my ability to be effective in those roles. In many ways, I am very grateful that I grew up in this type of AA household. That's the good news.

The bad news is that Dad seemed to use home as a place to recharge his batteries. When he was speaking at an AA meeting, he was "up" and "on" and "alive." Similarly, at home, when someone would call from AA, he would light up, and be full of all kinds of energy and enthusiasm. The rest of the time, however, he would sit and watch TV or sleep (at least, this is how I remember it). I have very few memories of him interacting with mom and me with the same enthusiasm or intensity that he gave to those he was helping in A.A. I never remember being upset about this. . . it just seemed to be "the way things were." Almost as if there was an unspoken rule that Dad's sobriety was essential for the stability of the family, and the way that Dad stayed sober was through A.A. Therefore, whatever supported this was essential.

Just to be clear, I want you to understand that I didn't, and still don't, see A.A., or Dad's involvement in A.A. as the problem. Quite the contrary, I see my exposure to the power of this twelve-step program as one of the most beneficial aspects of my childhood... one that continues to be a very positive influence in my work today and very congruent with my purpose (see Appendix III for more information on this positive effect).

What I am saying is that my memory of my father (and therefore my belief about what it means to be a father) was of someone who was very outgoing, nurturing, and supportive of those he came in contact with outside the family... and, somebody who used his home as a place to recharge his batteries, which means that he didn't give the same energy to his loved ones that he gave to others.

Of course, I never remember saying to myself, "That's how I am going to be when I grow up." However (as you might have guessed), as I entered my late twenties and early thirties, I found myself drawn to speaking and counseling (surprise, surprise). I even earned a master's degree in counseling psychology and was working toward my Ph.D., and . . . guess what? I found myself speaking to large groups of people with relative ease, and with a great deal of enthusiasm (just like my dad). In addition, when I was working with someone in counseling, I found myself very focused and enthusiastic about helping them (just like my dad). Then, I would go home and (you guessed it), recharge my batteries (just like my dad).

Finally, as my style of counseling, or my way of working with others, became increasingly focused on helping them be more purposeful in their lives, I began to examine my own life in terms of this paradigm (what a novel idea). As I did, I discovered this discrepancy. Clearly, following this old learned perspective of using home as a place to just recharge my batteries was incongruent with my purpose, a big part of which was to be a loving and present force in my relationship with my wife and children.

As I became aware of this, I was able to change ("Problems cannot be solved at the same level of awareness that created them." Albert Einstein). Now, when I come home, I purposefully give loving attention to my wife, Georgia, and my two sons, Chris and Nik. Not because "I'm supposed to," but because it's congruent with my highest purpose, and defines me in a way or makes a statement about who I am that I can be proud of. If I need to rest after a particularly exhausting presentation or trip, I say, "Dad needs a nap!" and I go take a short nap. You see, I still use home as place to recharge my batteries, I just do this in a purposeful way, or a way that is congruent with or how I want to define myself as a husband, father, speaker, and counselor.

That's the nice thing about becoming very clear about what our life would look like if we were living "on purpose." Once we have done this, we can use this vision as a criteria to determine which aspects of our past (which habits, learned perspectives, etc.) we want to hold on to, and which ones we want to let go of, or better yet change, so that our new habits are congruent with our highest purpose.

Just as I have a tendency to look forward to speaking in public versus fearing it, I'm sure that there are habits and learned ways of being that you want to hang on to as well. However, I think that we can all acknowledge,that there are also learned ways of reacting to life that do not serve us and that we would not like to hold on to and / or teach to those we love.

With respect to living life from the top of the mind, these less than desirable reactions can probably be seen on the right side of the Cycle of Stress.

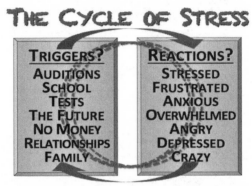

What it is important to recognize here is that these are learned reactions. We didn't come out of the womb reacting to auditions with anxiety and difficult people with resentment. Further, as we have already established, we didn't learn to react in these negative ways "on purpose." And yet, learn them we did. Therefore, unless we challenge them and change them, they will continue to influence our experience of life, even if that experience is negative.

The power of these old learned habits and perspectives was demonstrated very convincingly by Martin Seligman, Ph.D., a psychologist who was initially known for his work on the concept of what he called "learned helplessness."

In 1965, Seligman, while a graduate student in the department of experimental psychology at the University of Pennsylvania, performed the first experiment showing that animals can be taught "helplessness." One group of dogs was given an "escapable shock," meaning, by pushing a panel with its nose, any dog in that group could terminate or turn off the shock. A second group of dogs was given exactly the same shocks as the first, but they had no way to stop the shock and couldn't escape. A third "control group" was given no shocks at all.

Once the dogs went through the experiment, each was put in a large box with two compartments separated by a low wall. In the first compartment they received a shock, but they could easily escape the shock by jumping over the barrier into the other side of the box. Within seconds, the dogs that had learned that they could control the previous shocks jumped over the barrier and escaped. The dogs that earlier had received no shocks did the same thing, also in a matter of seconds. But two thirds of the dogs who had been taught that they had no control, that nothing they did mattered, made no effort to escape, even though they could easily see over the low barrier to the shockless zone of the box. Those dogs just gave up and lay down, even thought they were being regularly shocked by the box.

Dr. Seligman concluded that the reason two thirds of the dogs from the second group made no attempt to escape is because they had previously learned that they were helpless. Therefore, when they found themselves in a similar situation, they reacted based upon this learned perspective of helplessness versus jumping to the other side of the box.

Unfortunately, I think we all may have to deal with a bit of "learned helplessness," because there was a time in our lives when we were truly helpless. As children, there were many situations which we could neither change nor leave, and thus we may have some preconceptions about ourselves and the world that reinforce this helplessness rather than our power to change.

In fact, these old learned ways of responding aren't just thoughts, they are actual physical pathways in our brain. You see, whenever we think something, feel something, or do something, we create and/or reinforce what are known as neural pathways.

These conduits are similar to pathways in the woods in that, if they are new, they may be hard to find and go down. However, if we have reacted this way for a long time, the pathways are well worn, easy to find, and easy to go down.

That's why the reactions of stress, anxiety, frustration, and anger are so common and so easily triggered. The good news, however, is that we can begin to create and strengthen new neural pathways that go up to the neocortex versus down to the brainstem. These will be like new pathways in the woods at first. However, as we continue to practice thinking, feeling, and acting in ways that we would recommend to someone we love, we will begin to reinforce these new, more purposeful ways of being.

This is one of the reasons I have chosen to write this book, and the good news is that you have just taken a major step toward dispelling this old belief that nothing can be done (i.e. identified a more purposeful way of being when dealing with life's challenges). The bad news is that these will remain just good ideas, and eventually fade from awareness if we don't deepen our understanding of what actually causes us to think, feel, and behave the way we do and practice this new way of being. Put another way, if you want to have more influence over your emotions, behavior, and overall experience of life (and to some degree the emotions, behavior, and experience of others) then we need to understand the causal factors behind each.

CHAPTER 11

The True Cause of How we Think, Feel, & Act

M ost people think it's the facts, or what happens to us that makes us feel and act in certain ways. While the facts do play some role, I'm going to suggest that it's actually our piece of the P.I.E., or our Perceptions, Interpretations, and Expectations that are the most influential factors in determining our emotions, behaviors, and experience of life.

Let me give you an example. A long time ago, most people believed that the earth was flat. Based upon this perception, when a ship sailed out and didn't come back, most people thought that it had fallen off the edge of the earth. In other words, the prevailing perception of the world was that it was flat, and this influenced how the data (the ship not returning to port) was interpreted. Further, it's very likely that these same people would expect that if another ship sailed out too far, it would also fall off of the edge.

Here we have an excellent example of a perception or a belief coloring how data is interpreted, and the combination (of the perception and interpretation) creating an expectation about the future.

Staying with our example, when people thought that ships were falling off of the edge of the earth (based upon their belief that the earth was flat), and their expectation that this would continue to happen if the ships sailed out too far, they would very likely be afraid of sailing on ships, at least on the ships that were going to venture out of sight of the shoreline. Based upon this emotion (fear), they would understandably avoid ships (a behavior) which would produce a positive experience of feeling safe because they are not putting themselves in danger of falling off of the edge of the world. The graphic below demonstrates how this happens.

The facts (or what happens to us) are filtered through our perceptions or beliefs. These beliefs then create our interpretations which then create our expectations. Of course, because all of this happens so fast and outside our conscious awareness, we don't experience it this way. However, it is important to understand what is going on if we want to be able to influence the process.

Plus, as we have seen, when dealing with a perceived negative situation, the expectation that was created by our beliefs and interpretations is generally experienced as a worrisome image of some sort (such as ships sailing over the edge of the world, or our screwing up an audition). The reason this is important is that we have already learned that any image we hold in our mind produces certain chemical effects in our body, whether it's happening or not (remember the lemon?).

This is also why emotions are so hard to change. First, they (emotions) have been produced by perceptions and interpretations that we think are "true" (of course the earth is flat, of course auditions make me anxious, of course difficult people make me angry, etc.). Secondly, they create images of what we expect to happen next (I will be anxious until the cast list is out, I will either have to make the difficult person change or remove them from my life before I can find any peace of mind). We don't see the emotion as a result of the perception, interpretation, or expectation. We think it is being caused by the negative situation.

The ABC model developed by Dr. Albert Ellis can be helpful in understanding what is truly going on here. If we were to call the negative events and/or people in our lives, "A" (for the "adverse event") and how we react to theses events/people, "C" for the "consequences," we can see how most people believe that A causes C.

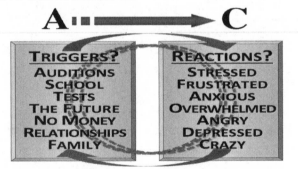

TRIGGERS?	REACTIONS?
AUDITIONS	STRESSED
SCHOOL	FRUSTRATED
TESTS	ANXIOUS
THE FUTURE	OVERWHELMED
NO MONEY	ANGRY
RELATIONSHIPS	DEPRESSED
FAMILY	CRAZY

Of course, the problem with this belief is that in order to feel differently, we must change "A," or somehow change all of the negative people and events to positive ones to ensure that they will no longer cause us pain. Suffice it to say, if you have made it this far in the book, you know that this isn't a viable solution.

In fact, we now know that the reason we have reacted with anxiety or anger in the past was because the middle part of our brain (our limbic system) saw (perceived/interpreted) these events/people as problematic or threatening. This interpretation threw our thinking into our brainstem, and we became trapped in the lower 20%, producing chemicals such as adrenaline and cortisol, and limiting our responses to fight-or-flight (the cycle of stress/frustration).

This awareness allows us to reject the premise that "A," or the adverse event causes "C," (the consequences). This is the good news because it means that we don't have to change "A," or the negative events in our life to be able to influence "C," (how we feel, think, or act). The reason that this is the case is because "A" doesn't cause "C". "A" is filtered through or triggers "B," and "B" causes "C," and, of course, "B" is our beliefs or perceptions (More on why this is the goods news later.)

Using the analogy introduced earlier, ships falling off the edge of the earth didn't cause people to be fearful of sailing. What caused them to be afraid was their belief that the earth was flat, and thus all ships that sailed out too far would fall off the edge.

A is Filtered Through B
& B Causes C

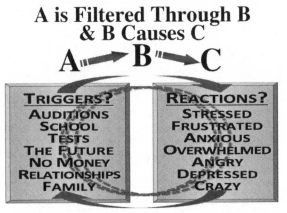

This is a relatively new (and some might even say radical) perspective, so let me give you another example of how this works. Let's say that we have three people in a room. The first was bitten by a dog when she was small, and has been afraid of dogs ever since. The second person in the room loves dogs. She has eight to ten dogs at home, and thinks dogs are some of the most loving of God's creations. The third person is from a country where dogs don't exist, and thus, he has never seen a dog before in his life.

You bring a dog into the room (fact). Predictably, you will see three very different reactions based upon three different sets of perceptions, interpretations, and expectations.

1. The person who believes that dogs are dangerous

interprets this as a dangerous situation. Her expectation is that she will be hurt. Her emotion is fear, and her behavior is to run from the room.

2. The person who believes that dogs are lovable joyfully exclaims, "A dog!" and goes over to pet and hug the dog. She interprets the situation as an opportunity to interact with one of her favorite animals, and her expectation is that she gets to be licked by the dog. Obviously, her emotion, behavior, and experience is positive.

3. The person who has never seen a dog before is confused, and just stands there wondering, "What the hell is that?" Not being able to draw any conclusions from his colleagues (one ran *away* from it, and the other ran *toward* this strange animal), he doesn't know what to do.

So, here you have a fact (a dog is brought into a room) triggering three different sets of interpretations, expectations, emotions, and behaviors. However, **IT'S THE SAME DOG!!!**, which means it can't be the situation, or the dog, that is causing the response. What *is* causing the reactions are the individuals' beliefs about dogs, and again, this is the good news. Why? Because, if our goal is to become more influential in how we feel, what we do, and generally how we experience life, we have much more influence over our perceptions and beliefs than we do any other aspect of the situation.

Unfortunately, this is not what most of us have been taught. Most of us were raised to believe that it's what happens to us (the facts) that cause us to react in specific ways, and thus we have been practicing or living by this belief for quite a while. In fact, many people have become so used to living this way that they are afraid of changing. They may even think of this way of life as a "comfort zone" from which they do not want to stray. However, if you have ever experienced the "cycle of stress/frustration," you know that it's not a very "comfortable" zone or place to be.

Still, you may know people who cling to the perceptions and/or beliefs that create this experience of life, even though the result is anything but comforting. There is a great quote by Michael Levine that explains this phenomena very well that says:

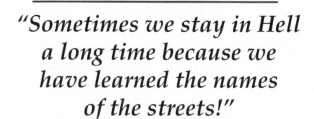

"Sometimes we stay in Hell a long time because we have learned the names of the streets!"
Michael Levine

I love this quote because it so succinctly explains why we keep doing the same thing over and over, even if doesn't seem to be working for us. We have "learned the names of the streets," meaning that this reaction has become so habitual and ingrained that we keep making the same judgements (which produce the same reactions), not because they are particularly comfortable or even effective, but because they are familiar and habitual.

In other words, it's not our "comfort zone" because it's not that comfortable. Instead, I call it our "known zone." It's what has become "known" or familiar, which explains why much of the material in this book, while compelling, might seem radical and even a bit unsettling to some because they have been taught to fear the unknown or unfamiliar.

By the way, have you noticed that the words "familiar" and "familial" are very similar? To be clear, I am not trying to blame our parents or our past for the habitual way we have learned to react to life. I just want you to understand why attempting to change these reactions, and shifting to a "Top of the Mind" perspective may seem awkward or hard at first. Just as learning any new skill, at first it will very likely feel unfamiliar. In fact, given the power of language, the word "unfamiliar" is a good way to describe the less than comfortable feelings (doubt, second guessing yourself, etc.), you may experience as you learn to live from the "Top of the Mind." Why? Because describing the experience this way automatically makes room for the fact that as we become more familiar with the process, it will seem more natural, and will eventually become a more purposeful habit. The challenge, of course, is to hang in there or practice this new way of being long enough for this to come to pass.

Of course, as mentioned earlier, we are always practicing something, and that's why this model for success begins with *clarity*... clarity about what we want to practice (our highest purpose) and what we don't, the old habits, beliefs, preconceptions, and / or learned perspectives that are incongruent with this purpose.

As we have discovered, the most powerful of these are our beliefs, for they give birth to everything else. In fact, the term "preconception" refers to a concept (belief) or conceptualization (way of interpreting or conceptualizing data) that has been conceived in the past (hence the prefix "pre."). Plus, the word conception means "to give birth." So, if we want to bring certain qualities to life, we must be very purposeful with respect to the concepts or beliefs that drive this creative process.

To make this decision, we must first be aware of the beliefs themselves, especially those that are associated with the aspects of our lives that in the past would have been defined as old triggers Therefore, I suggest that you take a moment and look at the list you made in Chapter Nine, i.e., those situations and types of people that have been problematic (or just make a new list now). Whether it was tests, auditions, the future, difficult people, traffic, your parents, or anything else that has seemed to "cause your stress" in the past, let's put them in their place and identify these as "A" or "the adverse event(s)." This will then allow you to identify "B," or the belief you have about these events or people, and "C" the consequence of holding on to this belief as valid, and allowing it to drive your thoughts, emotions, and behaviors.

To identify these beliefs, you can use this template and fill in the blanks:

In the past, I reacted to____A____ (the identified trigger, such as auditions, tests, difficult people, etc.) with___C____ (the old response, such as stressed, anxious, frustrated, etc.) because I was concerned or afraid that____B____ (your reasoning or rationale of the problem) might occur.

Or if you like, it could be written as, "In the past, when I faced____A____ (the trigger), I was concerned that____B____ (your worry or concern), which made me feel____C____ (the negative response).

Basically, anytime we can put, "I'm afraid that . . ." (or "worried that . . .," or "concerned that . . .") in any sentence, we know we are processing this information from the brainstem, and unless the situation is fight-or-flight in nature, we will not be accessing the most intelligent, purposeful part of our brain. Still, the first step to change is awareness of the causal belief or perception, and therefore we can use the template suggested earlier to understand how these old perspectives have affected us up until now.

For example, if someone found themselves feeling especially anxious about auditions, they might write:

"In the past, when I faced an audition (A), *I was afraid that* (B), *my not being chosen, would validate my fear that I'm not good enough, and so I felt* (C), *worried and stressed during the audition and afterwards until the cast list was posted.*

What this illustrates is a brainstem belief about auditions, i.e., that they are something to be feared because of their potential to make this person look bad or feel inadequate. While this belief may be common in young artists, it is just that, a belief, perspective, or preconception about auditions that is coming from the lower 20% of their brain. If it were a fact, everyone would experience the situation the same way.

For example, if anyone jumps off of a 20 story building without a parachute, they will fall and quickly come into contact with the ground, with rather disastrous results. This will happen no matter what the jumper believes about his or her ability to fly.

With auditions, however, this isn't the case. In fact, some people actually enjoy auditions because they see them as opportunities to perform. Their goal is to be cast in parts they enjoy and can really put themselves into, and therefore, they believe that if they enjoy the audition but don't get the part, this means that the director was looking for a different kind of actor, rather than seeing this as rejection and an indication of their lack of talent.

The only difference between the two scenarios is the way that the information is perceived or interpreted (which we now know depends on how the limbic system is processing the information). This is the power of beliefs, and why becoming aware of these perspectives is a key component to becoming influential in our lives.

Interestingly enough, many people resist this explanation and cling to the thought that, "No! It's the negative situations that make me feel bad!" And, of course, given the power of beliefs, if this is how they choose to explain or conceptualize their experience of life, then this will be true for them. Unfortunately, if they hold on to this belief, the only way they can change their experience will be to change the world around them, and they may find that many of the negative events and people in their life resist being changed. Plus, as we have learned, those who see problems as problematic and thus cause their limbic system to send the data to the brainstem and trigger worry and stress will quickly become trapped in this lower 20% of their brain, as well as be limited in their attempt to influence the quality of their lives.

As mentioned earlier, if we don't want to give negative events and/or people the power to "make us" feel one way or another, then we must take control of that power ourselves. The first step in this process is to see these negative reactions for what they are... chemical changes in our body that result from our becoming trapped in our brainstem. Next, we must be able to shift from our brainstem to the "top of our mind," and change the chemical makeup of our body. This is the function of the BRAIN model introduced in the first part of the book.

Having accomplished this, we must be willing to use life versus life using us, which means consulting our neocortex to determine how we want to define ourselves, or the statement we want to make about who we are when we are dealing with these challenging events and people. This means that rather than holding on to a belief that leaves us trapped in our brainstem, such as, "I am a person who becomes stressed when dealing with auditions, or frustrated around certain kinds of people," we can go back to the list of qualities and characteristics we came up with in Chapter Nine about the "Clarity of Purpose," and restate:

When I am dealing with _____,
I want to practice _____.

Or, we can actually put this belief in the form of a purposeful, self-defining statement by saying something like, *"I am a person who is practicing confidence* (or patience, or whatever quality you have chosen) *when dealing with difficult people, auditions, etc."*

Once we have this vision, and are willing to see the challenging situations in our lives as opportunities to practice, we must become aware of any old beliefs, habits, and/or preconceptions that are incongruent with this higher purpose. Remember the quote from Albert Einstein, *"Problems cannot be solved at the same level of awareness that created them?"* This means that we must raise our awareness as to whether the beliefs we have learned are serving us.

Again, one way to do this is to look at the negative reactions we have had to situations and/or certain types of people in our past, and determine what old beliefs/interpretations caused these reactions.

For example, we could say, "In the past, I became frustrated or angry with people who drove too slow or too fast in traffic because I was worried that _____ (they would keep me from getting where I wanted to go on time, they would cause an accident or were "beating me," and not playing by the rules, etc.) In this example, we can see how our beliefs defined us, because this tendency to react to slow drivers could also be stated as, *"In the past, I was a person who regularly became frustrated with people who drove too slow or too fast."*

Now we apply "<u>The Four Criteria</u>" to determine whether we want to hang on to this perspective:
1. Was this belief/reaction chosen on purpose?
2. Is it working for me?
3. Is this the statement I want to make about who I am in response to this situation?
4. Would I recommend this belief to someone I love?

As you can see, when this higher "Top of the Mind" criteria is applied, the answer is clear. Further, now we are in the position to create a new way of interpreting the speed people happen to be driving by stating: *"From now on, I am going to practice bringing the quality of* _____ *(serenity, acceptance, patience, etc.) to my experience of people who happen to be driving slower or faster than I am.* Or, *"I am practicing becoming a person who responds to slow or fast drivers with* _____."

In addition to the power of beliefs, there are linguistic forces at work here as well. I am a person who believes that the language we use to define ourselves and our lives has a powerful impact on our experience, and thus for those of us who want to maximize our ability to effect this experience, I suggest we use the proper tense in this description.

For example, some people will state, *"I really get anxious when I have an audition."* What is important to notice about this statement is that it is framed in the present tense. However, at the moment they aren't in an audition, and thus the statement isn't accurate. What they really mean is "in the past" they have become anxious when they were auditioning for a part. Notice the difference in these two statements? The second starts off with the words "in the past." Not only is this more accurate (in that it isn't happening in the present), these three words can actually pave the way for a more purposeful statement about who we want to be from this moment on.

In other words, the phrase, *"In the past, I had a tendency to become anxious in auditions"* makes way for something like, *"From now on, I want to practice patience, confidence, and creativity when auditioning for a part,"* or *"From now on, I am going to practice being a person who sees auditions as a place to practice doing what I love and defining who I am."*

Of course, these are my words, and the way you phrase the statement might be different. What's important here aren't the specific words, but (a) the tense we use to describe what is happening ("in the past" versus "from now on," and (b) the fact that we are making a purposeful statement about who we are, and what we want to practice.

For those of you who want to know how all of this works in our brains, let's go back to the illustration of the brainstem, limbic system, and neocortex. As we have discussed, data comes in through our five senses, and is first scanned by our limbic system.

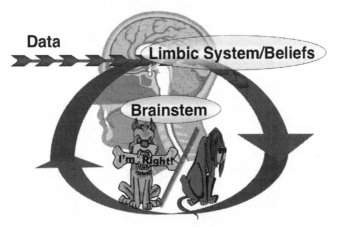

Because the limbic system is the part of the brain that is supposed to determine whether the data we are receiving is dangerous or some sort of a threat, this is also the part of the brain that holds our beliefs about exactly what is threatening and what isn't. Often, the criteria for this decision is determined by what we have found problematic or threatening in the past, and thus exists as a preconception. For example, the person who had been bitten by a dog is operating from the belief that dogs are dangerous (now and forever), and thus interpreted the fact that a dog had been brought into the room as a threat.

Again, this reinforces the power of our perceptions, interpretations, and expectations, and the importance of interpreting incoming data in a purposeful (versus habitual) manner. If our old beliefs about a particular situation and/or person are negative, the limbic system will immediately send the data about this stimuli down to the brainstem, bypassing our neocortex.

As we now know, this triggers a release of adrenaline, noradrenaline, and cortisol, which sends our body into a fight-or-flight mode. Further, because we then try to deal with whatever situation we are facing from this hypertensive state, we actually become less and less effective. This only increases our stress and frustration, and we become trapped in the brainstem.

There is a story you may have heard that illustrates how different parts of our brain can produce different experiences of life. It's about a little boy who was getting into a lot of fights at school. He was confused because a part of him believed that you should stand up for yourself, and not take any "lip" from anyone, while another part of him knew that fighting really wasn't the way to solve problems.

Unfortunately, he had not resolved these two perspectives, and thus was constantly getting into fights. Further, his teachers, and parents were becoming increasingly upset and concerned about the problem, and so finally the little boy went to talk to his grandfather. He said, *"Grandfather, I don't know what to do. I'm getting into a lot of fights at school, and part of me says not to take any lip from anyone while another part says that fighting isn't the way to solve problems. I am really confused."* His grandfather was very wise, and therefore, rather than lecturing to the boy, he told him a story about himself. He said, *"You know, I felt exactly the same way when I was your age. It was like I had these two dogs inside of me . . . one was a mean old dog, always looking to pick a fight, and the other was a more intelligent, even friendly dog, and they always seemed to be struggling for dominance."*

Upon hearing this, the boy's eyes lit up, and he said:

"That's it! That's it! Which dog won?"

The grandfather took a moment to let the message he was about to deliver sink in, and then very quietly said:

"It depended on which dog I fed."

I love this story because it reminds us that we are always feeding one of two perspectives. We are feeding the brainstem or our neocortex/Top of the Mind), and the dog that we feed, or the part of the brain to which we consistently send data will be the part of the brain that dominates our thinking and our life.

Or, put another way,

It's not what we *feel*, but what we *feed* that will determine our experience of life.

This is why we must be very purposeful about how we teach our limbic system to interpret the data we receive from our five senses, especially when dealing with the more "challenging" aspects of life.

For example, when we are studying for a test, rather than seeing this as a measure of our worth, or something we have to do well to get a good grade, we can ask, "what information on this subject would I like to be able to access in the future?" Even if it is information that isn't in our major, chances are we can become aware of how it can broaden our ability to understand a role, character, poem, joke, allusion, in the future.

The truth is, every time we learn something, we create a reference in our "library" (the upper 80% of our brain). This then allows us to draw upon this knowledge anytime we want to, and adds to the breadth of our creativity.

We could then see the test, not as a test of us but a test of the test. You see, a good test should accurately measure how much you know about a particular subject. However, it's very difficult to create a good test. It's easy to create a very hard test that almost no one does well on, or an easy test that everyone does well on. But a test that truly measures what a student knows is difficult to construct. Therefore, I always suggest that we first determine what we want to put in our library with respect to the subject matter, and then put our mind to learning that material. (Do you see how this is already a very different perspective on tests?)

When we are finished studying, we will have a pretty good idea of how much we have learned. Therefore, *I suggest you always give yourself a grade before you take the test!* You know better than anyone how much you know, and therefore are in the best position to give yourself a grade.

Next, as mentioned, you want to see the test as a test of the test. If you have learned 90 to 99 percent of the material, the questions on the test should simply remind you of what you know. I would encourage you to then imagine yourself taking the test, and each question sparking what you already know. It should be fun!

If it turns out that your actual experience of taking the test is less than positive, it's probably a flawed test. Regardless, however, you have stored this knowledge in your library and will have access to it for the rest of your life. And, isn't this the only real reason to spend time in a learning institution?

We've talked a lot about seeing auditions as an opportunity to perform versus an indication of your worth as a human being, or your future success in the arts. Remember, your ability to bring a character to life and bring your creativity to the process will rest on whether you are able to access the clear, confident, creative part of your brain. Fear of failure will block this access and trigger anxiety and chemicals such as cortisol.

Given that you are in the arts, you must love to perform, otherwise you might want to consider another field :) This means you very likely have many memories of being totally immersed in the joy of performing. As you think of these, can you see how different these memories are from the idea of auditioning? That's because many of us have learned to see auditions as a measure of our worth or talent, with the fear of rejection always looming in the back of our minds. This perception has become so entrenched, we don't even see it as a perception, but a fact ("auditions make me nervous").

Therefore, I encourage you *never to audition for anything for the rest of your life!* Instead, see the experience as an opportunity to do what you love, perform in a way that gives those casting the play, musical, film, etc., the opportunity to see if you fit the part. If you don't (fit the part) you would not want to be chosen because you would then have to spend countless hours doing something that isn't you, or being someone you're not.

In a recent interview, the multi-talented Mandy Patinkin speaks of the mistake he made in taking a role that he didn't like and wasn't right for him. He was originally chosen to co-star with Meryl Streep in the film "Heartburn," directed by Mike Nichols. However, only after a day on the set, he was fired and replaced by Jack Nicholson. Patinkin said that he knew that he wasn't right for the part from the first audition, but because he was ambitious and wanted to work with Streep and Mike Nichols, he took the part.

All of this is to say that given all the challenges of "the business," the joy of performing has been, and will continue to be our major payoff until we become successful, and even after. Therefore, let's look for any opportunity to experience this joy, even if it is only an audition. Given that when we are loving what we do, we have access to all of our talent and creativity, seeing the audition as an opportunity to experience the joy of performing, we also ensure that we are bringing our best to the role. Then, even if they don't see us as right for the part, they will see someone loving the art of performance, and who knows where that could lead.

By the way, Kaitlin Hopkins (Head of the Musical Theater Dept. at Texas State University and co-author of the foreword to this book) and I recently had the pleasure of presenting at a musical theater educators conference in New York City (The Musical Theater Educators Alliance or MTEA). During the conference, we heard William Wesbrooks, the Director of the Steinhardt School's Program in Vocal Performance at New York University, speak of his work described in his latest book, "Dramatic Circumstances: On Acting, Singing, and Living Inside the Stories We Tell."

He did some fascinating work with several students where he encouraged them to drop into their limbic system and brainstem from their neocortex in order to access those deeper emotions that can bring a performance to life. As an example, he encouraged one student who was singing "Maria" from West Side Story to access the danger and risk of rejection that falling in love can bring. And, because this vulnerability is indeed congruent with the experience, it resulted in the performance taking on deeper meaning and having a more profound effect on the audience.

I love this concept because of its purposeful nature. I also believe that the more influential we can be with our thoughts and emotions in life, the deeper we can go in our performances. We can allow ourselves to experience the vulnerability and risk of rejection in our roles because we have blended these more "dangerous" states of being into our lives in a way that is congruent with our highest purpose.

Just as our independence allows us to be more

interdependent without the fear of losing ourselves in our relationships, so can our ability to drop into our limbic system and brainstem from our neocortex allow us to experience intense and complex emotions (both in the roles we play, and in life) without the fear of being overwhelmed that these states may have triggered in the past. In other words, given that detached, or unemotional isn't how we want to be in life, (and is certainly not how we want to be as performers) we can experiment with bringing our vulnerability to life in a way that gives us the confidence to stay connected to our higher selves, even as we are accessing the lower parts of the brain. For more information on how this concept can be used to deepen the meaning and impact of your performances, I highly recommend Professor Wesbrooks' book, "Dramatic Circumstances: On Acting, Singing, and Living Inside the Stories We Tell."

Can you see how perceiving and interpreting situations in these new ways can support us in being successful? If so, I encourage you to apply this more purposeful way of seeing yourself and the world to everything you do.

Of course, this can be a tall order because, as mentioned earlier, this way of thinking is likely to be new and "unfamiliar" to most of us when applied outside the theater. In fact, for a while, it is very likely that we will still find ourselves reacting to the world in old ways in some situations. No problem... Following what we have learned, we can see this reaction as "good information," meaning that we can use the stress/frustration as a valuable signal. ("Stress is a signal something needs to change.") At this point, we can stop and allow our neocortex to regain control by taking three to five deep breaths and saying the word "relax" on the exhale, and ask the kind of "Top of the Mind" questions that allow us to access our best thinking, such as, "Who do I want to be (how do I want to define myself) in response to this situation? What are the old beliefs/interpretations that are causing me to feel frustrated? How is this data good information? What would I recommend to someone I cared for in this situation?

Then, having become clear about our purpose, our past, and our piece of the P.I.E., we can move forward, confident in the knowledge that the upper 80% of our brain is driving our thoughts, decisions, and behaviors, and that we are on our way to learning how to live "Life from the Top of the Mind."

Because this is such a new way of thinking and being, however, I want to give you as many tools as possible to support you in your success. Therefore, let's continue to add to this second model, which, if you remember, is designed to allow you to not only create a "Top of the Mind" perspective, but maintain it, even while dealing with life's most challenging situations.

CHAPTER *12*

Clarity About The Wisdom of Serenity

Of course, we are still talking about the value of the C^3 lifestyle, or how to bring clarity, confidence, and creativity to everything we do. Thus, the third step in this new model is called "Clarity About The Wisdom of Serenity." This concept should be familiar to you in that it was mentioned earlier in the book in conjunction with the word "Relax" in the BRAIN model.

If you remember, the "serenity" I am referring to here is based upon the "Serenity Prayer," attributed to the Protestant theologian, Reinhold

Niebuhr, which states, "God grant me the serenity to accept the things I cannot change, the courage to change the things I can, and the wisdom to know the difference."

Earlier, in Part One, the concept was included in the BRAIN model as a way to break the cycle of stress/frustration, shift from the brainstem to the neocortex, and change the chemical makeup of one's body. Part Two began with the clarity of our highest purpose, our past, and our piece of the P.I.E. This third step is designed to give us a concrete method of ensuring that we are in the most productive part of our brain, and are clear about where we want to focus our energy before we engage those "challenging" situations and/or people that in the past have been problematic. This step can also remind us of the value of shifting up into this higher-order thinking if we find ourselves trapped in the brainstem.

The Serenity Prayer suggests that when armed with serenity, courage, and wisdom, we are in the best position to effect change, or make the best use of our energy and efforts. Rather than continuing to rail against people and situations over which we have no control, we can accept these situations for what they are and focus our energy and attention on those aspects of life that we can influence or change.

Unfortunately, many people hold on to the belief that "acceptance" means to "give in," and thus feel defeated when they choose this way of relating to a person or situation. I believe that the exact opposite is true. From my perspective, "acceptance" in the context of the Serenity Prayer just means that we do not need some person or situation to change in order for us to respond to it on purpose. Therefore, rather than "giving in," it actually speaks to our independence, and removes a block to our being influential in defining who we are, regardless of the situation, and thus increases our power.

Of course, as the Serenity Prayer suggests, we must first access this state (serenity) in order to "accept the things we cannot change." Further, we must have chosen serenity and acceptance in order to have the courage to change the things we can (remember, serenity is the precursor to all acceptance, courage, wisdom, and change).

This makes sense if we look at the concepts of serenity, acceptance, courage, and purposeful change in terms of how our brain works, i.e., all of these qualities emanate from the "Top of the Mind." Therefore, if we are willing to create a purposeful sense of serenity, we will then be in the appropriate part of the brain to decide where to focus our energy, i.e., whether to accept what is happening and move on, or try to change it.

In fact, we can even use the prayer and the BRAIN model to cultivate "the wisdom to know the difference." For example, we can breathe deeply 3 to 5 times saying the word "relax" on the exhale, and then ask two neocortex questions:

1. *What about this situation will it take serenity for me to accept?*

Notice the difference between this question and the more common brainstem questions we may have asked ourself in the past when dealing with challenging situations, such as: *"What is wrong with these people?"* or, *"Why does this always happen to me?"* or *"Why do I have to change, they're the one with the problem!"* Instead, we can ask the neocortex question, *"What about this situation will it take serenity for me to accept?"* and this acknowledges the importance of deciding where to focus our energy in a particular situation, and uses the neocortex concept of serenity as a guide.

The answer could be the fact that traffic, other people, and logistics, such as, deadlines are situations over which we have no influence. If so, this will most likely take serenity to accept, which means we must cultivate this neocortex quality first in order to deal with these situations successfully. Or, put another way, rather than continuing to beat our heads against a wall trying to change a particular person or situation, we can choose to accept "what is" and move on, which frees us to focus on the aspect(s) of life that we can change.

However, often change takes courage, and thus we can use the "A" in the BRAIN model to also ask:

2. What about this situation will it take courage for me to change?

Of course, in order to change anything we must be able to influence it in some way, and the aspect of the situation over which we have the most influence initially is how we respond. For most people, however, it will take courage to first look inside and call upon the sort of qualities and characteristics that define us at our best before dealing with the situation at hand. Put simply, it will take courage to define ourselves first in a way that is congruent with our highest purpose before attempting to influence the world around us.

The good news, however, is that if we are able to follow the process suggested in the serenity prayer, i.e., cultivate a sense of serenity, accept what we can't change, summon the courage to change what we can, and then bring this more purposeful way of being to the situation, we will always be more successful. Why? Because this process ensures that we will be accessing our wisdom by coming from the most intelligent, capable, flexible, and skilled part of our brain... in other words, from the "Top of our Mind."

As you might expect, this, like any worthwhile endeavor, is easier said than done. In fact, most people will acknowledge that maintaining this higher perspective even for a day is challenging. Life seems to keep throwing road blocks in our way in the form of situations and/or people that can become triggers. In fact, many people would describe their day as an ever-escalating series of problematic events. They wake up in the morning, and it doesn't take long for some problem to pop up and begin the process. (See graphic below.) They put out one fire, and another seems to flare up unexpectedly which kicks their stress level up a notch. No sooner have they dealt with this problem when they are faced with yet another stressful situation, and once again their body is flooded with stress-related chemicals. By now, they are increasingly stressed, frustrated, and resentful of everything that has happened from the time they woke up, which, of course, limits their ability to deal with the next problem until finally, they just lose it.

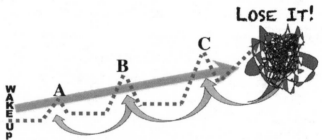

If you have ever experienced this sort of day, you know how problematic it can be, and how hard it is to change in the middle of "losing it." Most people will have to wait until that brainstorm passes before they can regain control (However, now that you know the BRAIN model, you are not like "most people!"). Still, it's important to know that it's easier to change at point "C" (before we lose it)...and even easier to change at point "B"... and even easier to change at point "A" ... because this let's us know that the sooner we catch ourselves and intervene, the easier it is to influence how we think and feel.

Of course, the easiest and most effective place to start is before the cycle of escalation even begins... i.e., when we first wake up. In other words, instead of waking up and having some person or situation start us on an ever-escalating tract to "losing it," we can ensure that our neocortex is in charge from the beginning (before we even get out of bed) by breathing deeply three to five times and saying the word "relax" on the exhale. Then we can ask the magic neocortex question: "What is my highest purpose this morning, say between now and lunch? I know some of the people I'm going to be interacting with, and many of the situations I will be in, so what are the qualities and characteristics I want to practice as I go into the morning?"

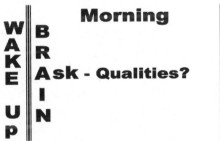

Once you have made the decision about

what you want to practice, you can now use your neocortex to create an image of going into the morning being this way. In other words, if you have chosen "confident" and "joyful" as who you want to be, what would it look like if you were being this way from the moment that you woke up? What would your morning routine look like, your breakfast, your trip to school, etc.

Because you have created this clarity prior to the event, you are in a much better position to actually pull this off. In other words, now that you are clear about this higher purpose, you can go into the morning confidently looking to practice this process of self-definition.

Of course, this doesn't mean that nothing will bug you. Remember, this isn't about being perfect, just purposeful. Therefore, when you notice that something or someone has triggered the release of adrenaline and cortisol, you can use this as "good information," and a signal that something needs to change. Further, since you now know how to change (the BRAIN model) and what to change (which part of your brain is driving your experience), you can breathe, say the word "relax" on the exhale, and ask yourself to recall the qualities and characteristics you defined earlier. You can then imagine yourself regaining control and once again bringing these qualities to life, and noticing the change. In fact, you may find yourself choosing to use the BRAIN model to allow the "Top of your Mind" to regain control several times during the morning. But hey, isn't that better than merely surviving, or worse, allowing these situations to continue to dominate your life?

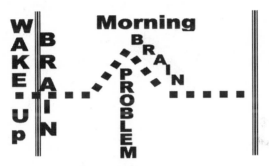

Now that you have used the morning as an opportunity for self-definition, sometime around lunch, you can stop and look back over the experience. What did you like about what you were able to accomplish? See anything you would have done differently? Given that this isn't about perfection, and that hindsight is always 20/20, it's often valuable to use this perspective to raise our awareness of what worked and what didn't.

Okay, now it's lunchtime, and you are about to go into the afternoon. If you want to continue to use life versus life using you, this would be a great time to define what you want to practice next. Again, you will likely know the sort of situations and people you will be dealing with in the afternoon, so, what is the statement you want to make about your character, or what is your highest purpose this afternoon?

Once this is decided, you then just go into this next part of the day using these situations to practice this self-definition. When something "bugs you," you can again use this as an opportunity to Breathe, Relax, and Ask the purposeful part of your brain what it wants to practice, Imagine bringing these qualities to life, and Notice the change. Even if you find yourself needing to do this more than once, it will still be a wonderful way to ensure that the most clear, confident, and creative part of you is running the show.

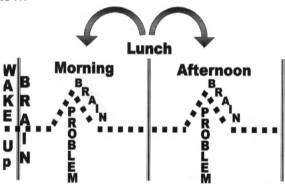

Finally, the afternoon is over and you are either driving home, or in some way transitioning between the day and the evening. This is a great time to look back over the day and use your perfect vision (20/20 hindsight) to determine if there is anything you would have done differently. The key to success here is to see all information as "good information" and use your neocortex to imagine more purposeful responses to any situations that may not have gone as you expected.

Then, after looking back, you can look forward. For those in the performing arts, the evening generally means rehearsals, performances, or hanging out with friends. Still, choosing who you want to be or the qualities and characteristics you want to bring to your evening activities is important because it allows you to go into these situations in the most purposeful way.

Of course, this doesn't mean all will be bliss. In fact, many people report that the hardest time to "keep it all together" so to speak, is when they are involved in theater activities. Therefore, if you find yourself triggered, you can still use life versus life using you, and take this opportunity to practice shifting from the brainstem to the neocortex by using the BRAIN model. Again, even if you have to go though this model several times over the course of the evening, you will merely be reinforcing your ability to use stress as a valuable signal, and shift to the "Top of your Mind" whenever you want.

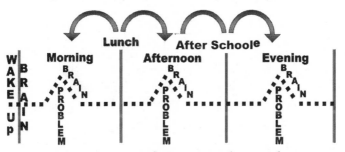

Okay, let's put this all together so that we can

see (graphically) how this information can help create and sustain a sense of purposeful serenity in our lives. As you can see in the graphic below, rather than life being a series of escalating events that result in our losing it, we can begin the day with the BRAIN Model and return to it as often as we wish.

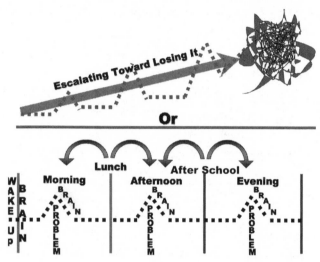

Plus, we are breaking the day into thirds, which allows us to focus on a few hours at a time and to use any situation that happens to arise (or that triggers a "rise" in stress-related chemicals) in order to practice responding in a more focused manner. Basically, we have turned the problem into part of the solution in that rather than trying to just "survive" the challenging aspects of our life, we have made them opportunities to practice shifting back to the "Top of the Mind."

The 2% Solution

Another aspect of success here is the ability to choose a pace of action that supports our desire to bring a "Top of the Mind" perspective to all we do. Unfortunately, many people are afraid that if they don't move quickly, they will not get everything done. We now know that this isn't the case, because we have learned that fear of anything throws us into the lower part of our brain. However, this doesn't mean that we won't find ourselves continuing to hurry through life trying to accomplish as much as possible in the shortest amount of time. As this quote (adapted from Sam Keen) says:

"We suffer from the illusion that the faster we run, the more likely we are to grasp happiness.
The truth is that the velocity necessary for success rarely exceeds the rate of reflection."

Adapted from Sam Keen

Therefore, in order to create the opportunity to reflect and / or think about what we are doing, and to take the edge off of the frenetic pace many of us have adopted as a way of life, I have created what I call "The 2% Solution."

The 2% Solution states that we can actually maximize our potential for accomplishment by doing everything we do 2% *slower!* The nice thing about changing our rate of activity by just 2% is that we will still accomplish what we want. It's just that if we are willing to do all of it 2% slower, we take the edge off of the frantic nature of the experience. Plus, the decision to move at this more purposeful pace comes from our neocortex, and thus continues to support our goal of living a more purposeful life.

Of course, all of this is about bringing a sense of serenity into your thought processes, and allowing this neocortex perspective to be a precursor for everything else . . . accepting what you can't change, changing what you can, knowing the difference, and of course, using life to practice defining yourself on purpose from a "Top of the Mind" perspective.

This is why being clear about this higher purpose, our past, and the wisdom of serenity is so important. However, given that life is so complex, I promised early on to give you everything I know about dealing with these complex situations. Therefore, let's move on to the last two steps, and complete the model designed to help you live "Life from the Top of the Mind."

CHAPTER 13

The Energy That Is Driving Our Thoughts, Emotions, & Behaviors

Obviously, everything that has been presented so far has to do with which part of our brain is driving our experience of life, with the goal of having the "Top of the Mind" be dominant whenever possible. In some ways, this chapter on energy is one of the most important in understanding and becoming skilled in bringing this perspective to life. However, due to the abstract nature of the concept of "energy," it is also one of the hardest to explain.

Of course, as with everything in this book,

the explanation begins with an understanding of how data is routed within our brain, the effects of this routing (which part of the brain is engaged) and the effects of the effects, meaning how all of this influences our experience of life. As we have learned, the limbic system is the gatekeeper, or the router, and when (based upon some old belief), this part of the brain interprets data as threatening, negative, and/or problematic in some way, it bypasses the neocortex and sends it down to the brainstem, which immediately goes into fight-or -flight.

In some very important way, all of this is dependent on the energy that is being used to decide whether the data is threatening or benign. On one level, this energy can be described as either positive or negative. In other words, when the limbic system is interpreting data through the filters of worry, stress, anxiety, etc., the brainstem will become engaged. However, when the limbic system is interpreting the same data as "good information," or a place to practice, the neocortex will become engaged. This is easy to see when we look at the energy behind the "reactions" in the cycle of stress, and compare this with the energy behind the qualities and characteristics you have purposefully chosen to make a statement about who you are, and who you are becoming.

Another way to understand this energetic force is to conceptualize it as either optimism or pessimism. Plus, both of the concepts of optimism and pessimism fit nicely within the models presented so far in that they represent ways of interpreting data that are based upon certain beliefs. According to the Encarta World English Dictionary, pessimism is defined as:

"A tendency to see only the negative or the worst aspects of all things and to expect only bad or unpleasant things to happen."

While optimism is defined as:

"The tendency to believe, or expect that things will turn out well" and/or "The attitude of somebody who feels positive or confident."

Can you see the basic beliefs underlying these different perspectives?

Of course, a pessimist would argue that pessimism is actually "realism," and that expecting the worst keeps them from being disappointed, and even allows them to be pleasantly surprised when something turns out well. While this may be true, I have a couple of problems with this perspective.

First, it would seem that in order to be "a realist," one must first be able to determine what is "real." On the surface, this might seem like a simple task, for all we have to do is look around us. What we can see, hear, touch, etc., is what is real and that's that. The challenge, of course, is that we only perceive a small fraction of the light and sound frequencies that exist (radio waves, spectrums of light, etc.). In other words, our five senses are not sensitive enough to hear, see, touch, taste, or smell what is really there, and thus, because we are not receiving totally complete and accurate information, we cannot rely on these senses to define reality.

I'm sure that there are some who might see this inability to determine what is "real" as a problem, however, I'm going to suggest that it's actually the good news! (Hey, I'm an optimist!). You see, one of the aspects of optimism that researchers have identified as responsible for the optimist's ability to deal with adversity and setbacks so successfully is that they are able to view the problem not so much as how things "really are," but as merely a temporary obstacle to their goal. Rather than see the situation as a failure on their part, or some confirmation of Murphy's law, optimists simply step back, reevaluate their options, and move on with the belief that they will eventually succeed. This means that their thoughts are on ways to succeed (neocortex) versus frustration and/or worry about the problem (brainstem), and because what we focus on expands, what is expanding are their options and strategies for success.

The second problem I have with the philosophy of "expect the worst and therefore you will never be disappointed" is that I wonder if the result is really worth the price? In other words, given that we now know the role beliefs, interpretations, and expectations play in creating our emotions, behaviors, and overall experience of life, if we are continually expecting the worst, our limbic system will always be "on guard," and thus will keep sending data down to the brainstem. This will, of course, limit our ability to respond to either fight-or-flight, which may not be the best way to deal with the situation at hand.

Plus, we now know that any image we hold in our mind changes the chemical make-up of our body (whether it's actually happening or not!). Therefore, given that any "expectation" is generally experienced as an image of what we expect to happen next, when that image is negative (i..e. when we expect the worst), we will be continually flooding our body with adrenaline and cortisol, which not only traps us in the brainstem, but also undermines our health, success, and well being.

If you remember earlier in Chapter Ten, "Clarity About Our Past," I told you of a psychologist by the name of Martin Seligman, Ph.D., and his research on the concept of "Learned Helplessness." Interestingly enough, he is also one of the world's leading authorities on motivation, and has done quite a bit of research on optimism and pessimism. These studies suggest that optimists are more successful than pessimists in almost ever facet of life... in school, in personal relationships, and even in the arts. According to Seligman, the reason for this success is because optimists persevere and are more creative in the face of adversity than pessimists. Plus, they have better physical health and may even live longer.

All of this makes sense given what we have learned about how positive and negative beliefs effect which part of our brain is engaged, and the type of chemicals that are released as a result. Further, it seems that this tendency to interpret data in an optimistic versus pessimistic way is not innate, but learned. This explains why Dr. Seligman calls his bestselling book on the subject, "Learned Optimism."

This is good news for those of us wanting to have more influence in our lives because if this is about how we have learned to interpret data in the past, we can now become more purposeful in this process of interpretation, and choose to see incoming data in a way that engages the most capable part of our brain. In fact, we can learn to do this even when (or maybe especially when) the data seems to be less than positive.

As a student in the arts, and as an eventual working artistic professional, your ability to stay positive (optimistic) while dealing with auditions, limited main stage roles, agents, canceled projects, and the unpredictable nature of "the business" is, and will be a critical factor in determining how you will experience this unique journey you have chosen.

Or, put another way:

"Optimism allows us to face the music, even when we don't like the tune."

In other words, even when optimists are not particularly happy with the "tune," or what is happening at the moment, they are able to "face the music" in such a way that allows them to change the channel or even rewrite the score. If this ability appeals to you, I suggest that we compose the music of our lives from a perspective that envisions the eventual success of both the composer and the composition.

Of course, even the most optimistic people experience stress and frustration from time to time, so let's see if we can view what some would describe as negative energy from a positive perspective, or at least see it as "good information." To do this, I want to offer a quote that came to me while working with a client. It says:

"Stress is an indicator of our belief in the value and validity of our worries and fears."

While some may view this as a statement about the problem, seen from a "Top of the Mind" perspective, it shows how even stress can be used to support a more purposeful way of being. For example, it states that stress is actually an indicator. Remember early in the book when I spoke of stress as a valuable signal..."Stress is a signal that something needs to change"? This is what I mean when I describe stress as an indicator of something. It is an indicator that we may be holding on to a certain kind of belief (or interpretation) that is being driven by the energy of worry and fear. In other words, to the degree we invest our worries and fears with value and validity (which means see them as both true and valuable, or helpful), we will experience negative stress. However, rather than making this just one more thing to worry about, we can see this stress as "good information," as an indicator that we are holding on to beliefs, interpretations, and expectations that do not serve us.

This brings a new level of awareness to the experience of stress (remember, "Problems cannot be solved at the same level of awareness that created them"). From this new perspective, we can now understand how the energies of worry and fear engage a very specific part of our brain and change the chemical make-up of our body. Given that this is often incongruent with what we want, we can change the energy we are using to drive/

create our state of mind. In fact, we can even use the BRAIN model to facilitate this change by first breathing deeply, saying the word "relax" on the exhale, and then asking the neocortex question, "What is the energy I want to choose to drive my experience of life at this moment . . . positive or negative, optimism or pessimism, worry or awareness?" If we choose to be positive, optimistic, aware, etc., then we can begin to practice using these energies to influence which part of our brain is engaged and to define who we are.

Unfortunately, some people have trouble with this more positive perspective, especially as it applies to people. They may feel that they have been open and trusting in the past, expecting the best from everyone, and that they have been let down, or even betrayed in some way as a result. Further, they may believe that if they let go of this sense of betrayal (i.e. forgive and forget), that it might happen again. Therefore, they hang on to the image of what happened and the pain it caused in order to keep themselves safe.

In my presentations, I generally illustrate this point by choosing someone from the audience and asking the group to imagine that I've been in a relationship with, or working with this person, and they betrayed and/or offended me in some way. At this point, I will walk up to the participant and ask him or her to stand. As they do, I will pick up their chair as a representation of the pain that they "caused me," and drape it over my shoulder, because, hey! I don't want them to think that it was "no big deal," and I certainly don't want them to think that they got away with it, or that they could do this to me again. I've got to protect myself somehow. So, I'm going to carry this grudge (their chair) as a symbol of what they did to me, and a reminder that I should never let this happen again.

Now I am looking for somebody very different from that last person to connect with so that I won't be let down like I was before. At this point (still carrying the chair), I will walk up to another person and speak of how nice they are and how I'm convinced that they won't hurt me, but guess what? They do! Here I ask them to stand and again take their chair as a representation of the pain that they caused, and as a reminder to not let this happen to me again. I continue this with two or three more people until I have chairs (my "protective" pain), draped all over me.

I then turn to the audience and ask, "Who wants to be in a personal or professional relationship with me now?" The point I'm wanting to make, of course, is that nobody can even get close to me because of all the pain/grudges I am carrying around. Further, rather than protecting me, what the pain is really doing is sapping my strength (it takes a lot of energy to continue to carry all this pain), as well as keeping me stuck in my brainstem and separate from my higher-order thinking.

Of course, the goal here is to introduce the energy of forgiveness as helpful and even necessary to living life from the "Top of the Mind." However, rather than seeing forgiveness as an energy that will set me up to be disappointed again, or a perspective that "let's them off the hook," I believe that it is instead a statement of self-definition. That's why I love the quote that states:

"Forgiveness is the realization that
you are no longer harmed."
Or
"Forgiveness is the decision that I will
no longer hold on to painful images of
the past to protect myself in the future."

Bottom line, if our goal is to create a purposeful life, at some point we must ask ourselves whether this tendency to hold on to the pain of the past as a way of protecting ourselves is really serving us. Is it really working for us to continue to define ourselves as "harmed" in order to stay safe . . . . is it congruent with our highest purpose?

The truth is that forgiveness, or our "forgiving" another (or even ourselves) has nothing to do with letting anyone off the hook. What it's really about is making a purposeful choice about whether we are going to use the pain of the problem (and a vision of ourselves as harmed by that pain) as a way to protect ourselves in the future. If this seems incongruent with your vision of life, you might consider letting go of that pain and creating a vision of yourself as "no longer harmed." So, now we can add "forgiveness" to the energies of awareness and optimism as examples of drivers that should support your decision to approach life from the "Top of the Mind."

There is one more concept I'm going to suggest before we move on to the final step of this second model. This suggestion is specifically for those of you who would define yourselves as perfectionists. First, let me say that I understand and admire the drive of a perfectionist. These are generally people who are very conscientious and have a deep desire to do and be their best. In fact, they may believe that if you are not going for perfection, it means that you just don't care, and these people care quite a bit.

The problem with expecting perfection from yourself and others, of course, is that "perfect" is rarely (if ever) achieved, and thus you are setting yourself and everyone else up for failure. So, what energy can we choose that is both achievable and ensures that we will bring our best to life? I suggest the energy of excellence, especially as it is defined in this quote from Ronnie Max Oldham:

Excellence is the result of:
__Caring__ more than others
think is wise,
__Risking__ more than others
think is safe,
__Dreaming__ more than others
think is practical, &
__Expecting__ more than others
think is possible.
Ronnie Max Oldham

I see this as an "excellent" quote and perspective for several reasons. First, there is a clear message here that who we are and how we approach success cannot be based upon what others think. In other words, while some people might tell us not to care, risk, dream, or expect too much from ourselves or others, we don't have to follow their advice. In fact, according to Mr. Oldham, it is our willingness to reject these limitations and care, risk, dream, and expect more than others that will determine the degree to which excellence is the driving energy in our lives.

Second, when we go for excellence versus perfection, we not only set an attainable goal, we don't limit where we can go after the goal is reached. With perfection, once it is attained, there's no way to improve. You can't become "more perfect." With excellence, however, we can always become more excellent or increase our ability to care, risk, dream more than before. Therefore, since success is always about continual improvement, I am recommending excellence along with awareness, forgiveness, and optimism as choices for what energy drives our thoughts, feelings, and decisions.

Bottom Line: Don't use the Energy of the Problem to Create the Solution!

The important thing here is to choose a neocortex energy if you want to live life from the "Top of the Mind." While this statement would seem to be common sense, unfortunately it isn't common practice. In fact, most people do exactly the opposite. They become stressed and frustrated, and then they attempt to use this energy to solve the problem. This means that they run the problem over and over in their heads until their worries or concerns motivate them to take some action.

We now know why this rarely works. The experiences of stress and frustration are first generated by the brainstem. These negative emotions then re-engage this lower 20%, thus limiting our ability to access the most intelligent, capable part of our brain. As stated earlier, the energy of the problem can not/will not create a solution, and thus, we always want to first choose an energy that is more congruent with our highest purpose, or what we want (versus what we are afraid of) as a creative force.

As promised, here is a way to use the BRAIN model to choose and install such an energy. We can ensure that our neocortex is in charge by going through the first two steps (breathing deeply and saying the word "relax" on the exhale), and then we can ask the neocortex question:

"What is the energy I choose to drive/influence my thoughts, emotions, and behavior in this situation?"

Or, we can use the Four Criteria to evaluate and, if necessary, change the energy that is driving our life. For example, we can ask:

1. Was this energy chosen on purpose?
2. Is it working for me?
3. Is it helping me make the statement I want to make about who I am?
4. Would I recommend or teach this energy to someone I love?

If the answer is "No," then we can choose an energy that would meet these criteria: i.e. that is chosen on purpose, that does help us create the experience of life we want, that does make the statement we want to make about who we are and finally, that we would recommend to those we love. We can then imagine bringing this energy (awareness, confidence, excellence, love, forgiveness, etc.) to life and notice the change, or become clear about how this way of being might be different from how we might have dealt with this situation in the past.

Of course, you don't have to limit yourself to the energies I have suggested. You can choose anything you want. You must, however, choose an energy deliberately, or "on purpose" because otherwise these choices will be made for you by your habitual beliefs formed in your past.

CHAPTER 14

The True Meaning
of
Responsibility

If you remember, we are talking about the value of the **C³** lifestyle, or how increased Clarity, Confidence, & Creativity will help us live "Life from the Top of the Mind." So far, we have discovered the importance of coming from a specific part of our brain and being clear about:

• Our highest purpose,
• Our past and our piece of the P.I.E.
• The wisdom of serenity, and
• The energy that is driving our thoughts, emotions, and behavior.

To complete the model and give you all of the tools you need to bring more confidence and creativity to everything you do, we must also become clear about the role "responsibility" plays in our lives. While this would seem to be obvious, (who doesn't think that people should be more responsible?) have you noticed that the act of "taking responsibility" is becoming a lost art? Cries of "Not my fault," and / or "I'm not responsible" seem to be much more prevalent today than, "I take full responsibility for how I responded to this situation."

Why do you think this is? If the quality of responsibility is so universally admired, why do fewer and fewer people want to claim this as a defining characteristic? I believe the reason behind this refusal is that many people see the act of taking responsibility as dangerous. They are afraid that if they take responsibility and something goes wrong, then they will be to blame. As we have learned, any time we perceive anything as dangerous, our limbic system sends that data to the lower 20% of our brain, and thus, we will interpret our taking responsibility as a potential threat.

Given our recent understanding of what is happening here, I suggest that we draw upon what we have learned in step two of this model (Our Past and our P.I.E.) and change the belief or perception that is causing this response (which will, of course, change the response). In other words, if our old interpretation/belief around the concept of "taking responsibility" isn't serving us, I suggest we replace that perception with one that is congruent with the statement we want to make about who we are, and who we are becoming. I suggest that we make re-responsibility less about, "Who's to blame" and more about our "ability to respond"

Response-ability... Our Ability to Respond

Further, if our goal is to be able to respond to life in a way that is congruent with our highest purpose (the qualities and characteristics we identified earlier), then I suggest that we take 100% responsibility for our ability to respond!

To be clear, this doesn't mean that we should now become responsible for everyone else. Taking 100% responsibility for our ability to respond simply means that we are not going to wait for some situation or person to change before we decide who we want to be in response.

In fact, drawing from the material presented in Chapter Nine (Clarity of Purpose), we are moving beyond simply "not needing something to change." We are actually using the situation to define who we are. Of course, as mentioned earlier, this is easier said than done. However, if our goal is to become more influential in every aspect of our lives, and operate from the Top of the Mind," this will only be possible if we are taking 100% responsibility for how we respond to the challenging aspects of life, versus blaming other situations and/or people for what we think, feel, and do.

For those of you who have found the BRAIN model helpful in accessing your neocortex and making the most of each step in this second model, we can continue that process here. For example, as you have done with the four earlier steps, you can breathe deeply, say the word, "relax" on the exhale, and ask the magic neocortex question:

"If I were taking 100% responsibility for my ability to respond to _____ (whatever situation you happen to be dealing with at the moment), *what would that response look like? How would I be thinking, feeling and acting differently?"*

Then, you could imagine responding to life in this new, more "able" manner, which not only has your body changing chemically as if the experience were real, but also gives you a clear vision of what you want to practice. You then can notice the change you have produced in yourself and go into life noticing the changes in who you are, and how this more purposeful, "Top of the Mind" way of being effects everything you do.

As mentioned earlier, I like the models that I create to spell something meaningful so that they are easier to remember, and also reinforce the material introduced. Therefore, this second model spells POWER (Purpose, Our Past / P.I.E., Wisdom of Serenity, Energy, and Responsibility) because it is designed to help us become more influential and / or powerful in our lives, and to some degree, the lives of others.

Further, as we combine the POWER model with the C^3 model, we can begin to see how each model supports the next.

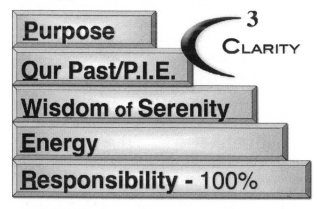

For example, in terms of *clarity*:

• When we become clear about our purpose or what we want to accomplish, and our highest purpose, (or the statement we want to make about who we are) and purposefully or deliberately bring this sense of clarity to every situation, we become more powerful.

• When we become clear about our past and own our piece of the P.I.E., meaning the old habits, learned reactions, and / or preconceptions that are incongruent with this higher purpose, we can change the perceptions, interpretations, and expectations that are driving these habits to ones that support the statement we want to make about who we are, and we become more powerful.

• When we become clear about the wisdom of serenity, or the value of using serenity as a precursor to accepting what we can't change so that we have the courage to change those aspects of our lives over which we have the most influence, we become more powerful.

• When we become clear about the type of energy we want to drive this process (awareness versus worry, excellence versus perfection, love versus fear), and actively choose this energy to motivate our thoughts, emotions, and behavior, we become more powerful.

• And finally, when we are willing to take 100% responsibility for our ability to respond so that we need nothing to change in order to practice this "Top of the Mind" perspective, we become more powerful.

Clarity Creates Confidence:

With this clarity of purpose, our past/P.I.E., the wisdom of serenity, energy, and the importance of responsibility, we are able to go into any situation with confidence, because we will know why we are there and what we want to accomplish (i.e. using life versus life using us to make a statement about who we are).

Without this clarity, however, we will just continue to react to life as we have in the past. Of course, this too can be "good information," for when we find ourselves caught in this old cycle, we can excuse ourselves and use the BRAIN model to break the cycle by shifting from the brainstem to the neocortex and changing the chemical makeup of our body. We can then become clear about our purpose, our past/P.I.E., the wisdom (importance) of serenity, the energy we want to use, and our willingness to take responsibility for it all, and this will allow us to re-enter the situation with the confidence of a "Top of the Mind" perspective.

Clarity & Confidence Allow Creativity:

Of course, this isn't to say that just being clear and confident will always result in success. Life is almost always more complicated than we expect, and thus we will need to be very creative in how we deal with each situation. The good news is that this creativity (which is, of course, a "Top of the Mind" neocortex quality as well) will be much more accessible when we begin with the sort of clarity and confidence I have described, and when we continue to remain in the upper 80% of our brain.

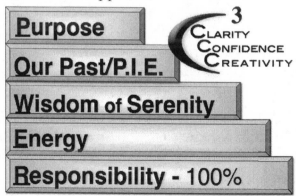

The best way to do this is to ensure that the data we receive is continually sent up to the neocortex rather than down to the brainstem, and the best way to do that is to interpret this data "on purpose," almost as if it is being filtered through our clarity, confidence, and creativity. Again, this is the "good information" versus the "ain't it awful?" perspective which allows us to see the incoming data in terms of awareness versus worry. This ensures that the data is sent up to the neocortex and then recycled through the limbic system.

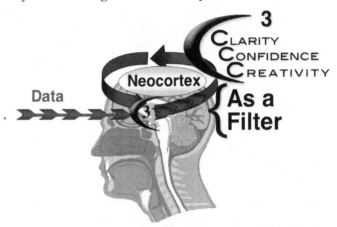

The reason I point this out is that some people are concerned that this "Top of the Mind" perspective is just about being "intellectual," as if there is no emotional component in the model. While this is understandable, it couldn't be further from the truth. I believe that emotions are a vital part of life, especially the sort of fulfilling, meaningful life that

I have been alluding to in this book.

In fact, as a person who attempts to practice what I preach, in my work as a psychologist and public speaker (as well as my other roles as a father, husband, and friend) I bring a LOT of emotion to who I am and what I do. It is the quality of our emotional experience (and how this experience affects the quality of our lives), however, that should, in my humble opinion, be chosen "on purpose."

In other words, given what we have learned about how our emotions are created by the beliefs and perceptions we hold about ourselves and the world, and further, that these beliefs determine how we will interpret the data we receive and what part of our brain will be engaged as a result, my suggestion is that rather than allow old preconceptions to continually send this data down to the brainstem, we should instead choose to see the data as good information, and thereby engage the Top of our Mind.

Then, from this more purposeful perspective, we can re-engage our limbic system in such a way that we can influence what emotions we bring to life. This creates a cycle that serves our higher purpose and allows us to continually re-engage the most intelligent, capable and purposeful part of our brain.

Okay, now we know what the problem has been and what we can do about it. We have learned how to see situations such as deadlines, auditions, and traffic as opportunities to practice living "life from the top of the mind," and have been given several models to support this process. Let's move on to see how all of this information can be applied to what many have said is the most challenging of situations... dealing with difficult people.

However, before we go there, let me make one suggestion. You might want to stop reading for a short while (a week or two should suffice), and practice applying what you have learned to some of the more "static" triggers, such as deadlines, auditions, school, etc., before attempting to use this philosophy with the difficult people in your life.

One reason for this suggestion is that it is easier to practice defining oneself on purpose and to engage the "Top of our Mind" when there is only ONE brainstem involved. Difficult people bring their own beliefs, preconceptions, worries, and concerns to the encounter, and this extra brainstem energy can make dealing with these individuals extra challenging.

It would most likely serve you, therefore, to first become skilled at changing the chemical make-up of your body and shifting to the "Top of the Mind" in situations that don't directly involve other people before moving on.

Part III

CHAPTER 15

Dealing with People "On Purpose"

I am going to frame this material on becoming more influential with others in terms of some of the more challenging or difficult individuals that we encounter, because most everyone tells me that it is these "difficult" people that have triggered the most negative reactions. In other words, even when we had a disagreement with someone, if they were willing to sit down with us and discuss the situation, it didn't necessarily turn into a problem. However, when "the other" responded by being defensive, angry, argumentative, or even just resistant to our point of view, often this resulted in a negative reaction on our part as well.

As you might imagine, the way the "Top of the Mind" philosophy conceptualizes the problem of difficult people is congruent with its conceptualization of problems in general. External stimuli (in this case, difficult people) have been perceived by our limbic system as threatening, dangerous, and/or problematic in some way, which has resulted in the lower part of our brain becoming engaged, and certain chemicals being released in our body. Or put simply, in the past when we were dealing with people who were argumentative, stubborn, defensive, angry, arrogant, etc., we tended to respond in kind, i.e. we became defensive, resentful, insistent, and even angry and stubborn as well.

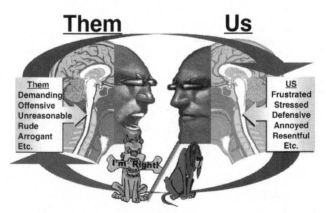

This created the now familiar cycle (in this case, the cycle of conflict/resistance) which resulted in our becoming trapped in the brainstem.

While similar to the cycle of stress, unfortunately, the cycle of conflict/resistance creates unique and often more problematic results. When we find ourselves becoming frustrated with tests or deadlines, the problem is generally limited to ourselves and our experience (school only seems to get worse rather than actually reacting to our reaction.) Difficult people, on the other hand, will almost always react to our reaction! Because they are coming from *their* brainstem, they predictably become more defensive, resistant, angry, stubborn. etc. This negative reaction shuts down communication, and often disintegrates into an argument about who's right, who's to blame, and who needs to change.

Further, the ramifications of this negative interaction are rarely limited to the moment. The energy behind this interaction can stick with us throughout the day or even the week, and color our mood and/or mind in such a way that limits our ability to access our best thinking. Plus, this sort of encounter can also color how we interact with the difficult individual in the days and weeks ahead. Rather than creating a future environment of cooperation, or even starting our interactions with this person with a blank slate, we instead begin with one foot stuck in the brainstem.

In addition, because they have labeled us as the difficult person, they are often motivated to go and tell someone else about the incident. This "someone" could be another person in our class, their best friend in the program, our professor, or anyone they think will agree with them, or anyone who is in the position to make us pay for "how we treated them."

Of course, this rendition (which generally begins with, "You would not believe what so-and-so just said/did to me!!") is from their point of view, and thus we come off looking like some irrational deviant that is obviously wrong. Now we have the added problem of having to deal with the fallout from their rendition. This could include our being seen by others in a negative light, explaining to our professor what went wrong, or simply having to deal with the fact that we now have a "resistant relationship" with this person that will make future interactions even more difficult, not to mention the stress and frustration we are experiencing as a result of the original conflict.

Needless to say, when the "cycle of conflict/ resistance" becomes our relationship with this person, something needs to change. Unfortunately, most people see the difficult person as the cause of the problem, and thus try to change "them." On one level, this makes sense because we "know" that if they would just stop being so difficult, we could reason with them and work toward a solution. The problem, of course, is that difficult people will almost always interpret any attempt to change them as criticism, and react by becoming even more resistant.

In my seminars, I demonstrate this phenomena by pairing up the participants, and randomly assigning them to be either "A" or "B." I then instruct "A" to make one of their hands into a tight fist. I then tell the "B's" that they have thirty seconds to get "A" to open their fist ANY WAY THEY CAN!!!!! As you might imagine, this results in a chaotic scene where the "B's" try to force their partners to open their fists while the "A's" react by increasingly tightening their grip and resisting with all their might. After thirty seconds, I stop the exercise, and determine what percentage of the group were able to get their partners to open their fist.

While the numbers vary somewhat depending on the makeup of the audience, the percentage is never more than 30%, and often as low as 0%. The reason for this is that the most popular strategy used by the "B's" is the "force and pain method," which is just what it sounds like, i.e., trying to pry their partner's fist open using physical force.

I then ask *all* of the participants to make a fist and imagine that someone is trying to force them to open their hand, and ask them what their reaction would be. They all say that they would resist by tightening their fist or striking out at the person trying to get them to change. Of course, this is what I am wanting them to understand, i.e., when we try to force another to change, what we are actually doing is motivating them to resist us even more!

I call this the "Lesson of the Fist," and it may be one of the most important concepts to learn if maintaining a "Top of the Mind" perspective and becoming more influential with others is one of your goals.

The Lesson of the Fist

What this means, of course, is that in order to deal with difficult people successfully, we can't try to change them first. Because they are trapped in their brainstem, they will interpret any suggestion that they should change as criticism, and as a result become even more resistant. Or, as the "Lesson of the Fist" says:

Whenever we try to force anyone to change, they will either resist us or resent us or both, and as a result become more motivated to defend their position!

So, what can we do? Well, first I suggest we

ensure that we are coming from the part of our brain where we have access to our best interpersonal and problem-solving skills. Otherwise, we will just be two people battling brainstems. The best way to do this is to use any feeling of "stress" (frustration, anger, annoyance, etc.) as a valuable signal that we are coming from the lower 20% of our brain, and use the BRAIN model to shift to the neocortex, or "Top of the Mind." This means becoming very aware of how we are reacting to difficult people, and being willing to stop the interaction and make this shift before we attempt to solve the problem.

The challenge is to do this (stop the interaction) in such a way that they don't feel as if their issue(s) are being dismissed or "blown off." Often, this can be accomplished by just excusing yourself to go to the bathroom. Here you can practice the BRAIN model, and return having engaged the most clear, confident, and creative part of your mind.

Okay, we now know that if we try to force others to change (or even suggest that they are wrong), this will only drive them deeper into their brainstem and motivate them to "tighten their grip" and resist us even more. In addition, we know that in order to be successful with these resistant individuals, we must have shifted from our brainstem up into our neocortex so that we have access to our best thinking and our clarity, confidence, and creativity.

Finally, we also know that we don't want to

be continually falling back into the brainstem and having to shift up into the neocortex, but instead, we want to find a way to come from this upper 80% consistently, especially when dealing with difficult people and situations. Therefore, the next section explores how the models presented earlier support this consistent "Top of the Mind" perspective, and additionally, how to motivate others to shift to the most receptive part of their brains and bring their best to the discussion as well.

CHAPTER *16*

Difficult People &
Our Highest
Purpose

A s in Chapter Nine, "Clarity about our Purpose," this first step is designed to ensure that (a) we have chosen our response deliberately or "on purpose," (b) that this response is congruent with the statement we want to make about who we are, (c) that these choices are being made by our neocortex versus our brainstem, and (d) that these choices are also congruent with the effect we want to have on the interaction.

Notice that I positioned "the effect we want to have on the interaction/other person" last on the list. Why? Because this is often the first and only thing people want to accomplish when dealing with others. They want to either prove them wrong, or at minimum, change them in some way, (i.e. make them stop being so difficult!).

While this is understandable, we now know that even if we are "right" and/or even if our desire to change them is benevolent, they (these difficult people) will very likely respond to our efforts by redoubling their opposition. Therefore, this desire to influence them must be our last consideration if we wish to be successful.

In fact, even before we explore how to be influential with people, we must first determine how important this person is in our life. In my master classes, I illustrate this concept by asking participants to imagine a difficult person that they have encountered that they don't know well (or don't know at all). This could be a driver who cut us off on the freeway, or a rude customer service agent, or even a student from a class that we don't know. I ask, "On a scale from 1 to 10 (with 10 being the most), how important do you want this person to be in your life?"

The answer I receive most often is "0," which certainly makes sense. However, if we define "important" as who we allow to change the chemical make-up of our body, there are two ways to make someone important.

+10
+9
+8
+7
+6
+5
+4
+3
+2
+1
0
-1
-2
-3
-4
-5
-6
-7
-8
-9
-10

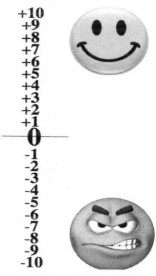

We can love them and that makes them important. Or, we can resent them or be angry with them, and that also makes them important. In other words, when we get upset at bad drivers, rude service people, classmates, or others that we don't know or at least don't know well, *we have made them the most important person in our life!*

What's the alternative? Well, if we truly want them to be a "0" or minimal in terms of importance, we need to become clear about how we relate to people who have little to no importance in our lives. Chances are this means we might notice their behavior, but we don't take it to heart, or make it something we get upset over. In fact, we probably don't give it a second thought.

On the other hand, if the person is a classmate,

or someone we will be interacting with in the future, then this makes them a bit more important. And, given how our career in the arts can be affected by how people see us (whether they want to work with us, recommend us to others, etc.) then we may want to be as influential in these relationships as possible without having them dominate our thinking.

And, of course, if this is one of our best friends, or someone we are in a relationship with, then obviously this person is very important. The value of making this determination is that we now have some idea of the time and energy we want to put into influencing this relationship. Dealing effectively with others (especially those who are upset with us or resistant to us) takes a lot of skill and energy, and if we try to become influential with every difficult person we encounter, we quickly become exhausted.

Okay, let's assume we have decided that the person in question is indeed important enough for us to spend our time and energy on. I do plan to give you a model for becoming more influential with these people. However, we will not be able to use this model successfully until we have shifted to the "Top of our Mind," chosen our response from this upper 80% of our brain, and made practicing this response our highest purpose, or the most important thing we are doing.

In order to make this process powerful and

relevant to your life, I suggest you once again get a clear picture of the situation, i.e., first make a list of the types of difficult people you have found to be most troublesome. Then, across from each, note the quality and/or characteristic you want to practice when you next encounter one of these people.

Feel free to consult the list you made in Chapter Nine, for you may find that some of the qualities you defined there are also ones you would choose in the sort of specific situations we are describing here. However, don't feel you must limit yourself to these qualities, because you may also discover that there are some very specific qualities that you want to practice with specific types of difficult people.

For example, you might decide that when dealing with people who are stubborn, you might want to practice *patience* or *curiosity*. Or, when dealing with people who, in the past, have triggered feelings of intimidation, you might want to practice *confidence*.

There is, of course, no wrong answer here. The only requirements are that this list be made, and that the qualities chosen be positive versus "less negative" (unafraid, less angry, less intimidated, etc.) because, as we have learned, until we have a clear, positive, vision of who we want to be, what we want to practice, and/or the statement we want to make about ourselves in these situations, we will remain at the mercy of our old habits and brainstem reactions.

Now that we have defined what we want to practice, the challenge is to imagine using these encounters to bring these qualities to life. This can take place first in our mind, which means that it is very likely that we will be successful because we are controlling all aspects of the situation with our imagination. This isn't a problem unless we imagine the difficult people changing so that we feel better. We may not want them to be that powerful in our lives, and, even if they are important, we don't want our ability to choose our response to be dependent on them changing. Or, put another way, **You never want to tie your peace of mind to another's state of mind.** Therefore, for the moment, just imagine them being as difficult as they want while we are practicing our chosen response.

This is similar to the imaginary island and the "difficult individual" I spoke of in Chapter Nine where we discussed hiring an actor to play their part while we practiced responding "on purpose," and decided to just use the "real life" difficult person for free!

Basically, the idea is to create an imaginary scenario where the environment was created specifically for us to practice. The value of this exercise is that (a) we have drawn information about who we want to be from the "Top of our Mind" versus just talking about being less reactive, (b) rather than worrying about them and thus making them the problem, we are making them part of the solution by using their behavior as an opportunity to practice, and (c) this process gives us a chance to create this image first in our mind where we have the ultimate influence. This is important because the first step in accomplishing anything, especially anything as intense as dealing purposefully with difficult people, is to first be able to imagine ourselves doing it successfully.

Of course, as you might imagine, actually being able to respond this way in "real life" is quite another matter, and that's why this is only the first step in the POWER model. Further, I promised an additional model that will help you become more influential with these difficult people by actually motivating them to shift from their brainstem up into their neocortex.

The problem, as I have mentioned, is that many people want to do this first (changing the other) and now we know why this will never work. In fact, in order to put ourselves in a position to be influential with others, we must do much more than just imagine it happening, so let's continue on and discover how the POWER model supports us in this process.

CHAPTER 17

Difficult People, Our Past, and Our P.I.E.

As we have learned, we don't come to these encounters as blank slates, but instead, we bring a whole host of learned beliefs, habitual responses, Perceptions, Interpretations, and Expectations to the experience. In addition, the difficult person also brings their own learned perspective or "piece of the P.I.E." to the encounter, and this is one of the reasons why interactions such as these can be so volatile. Therefore, if we want to be able to influence our emotions, behavior, and experience with these individuals, as well as have some influence over their emotions, behavior, and experience, we must be very clear what creates these aspects of life. As we learned in Chapter Ten, it is not just the "fact" that someone is upset with us that causes us to react in old, defensive, and/or offensive ways, but our belief about what this means (interpretations) and our expectations about how it will effect our lives.

Therefore, in order to be successful in situations such as these, we must first ensure that we truly understand this creative process, and have chosen how we want to use this model to support our goals. Let's begin with "them." In other words, if their difficult emotions and behaviors are being driven by certain beliefs about themselves and the world, I suggest that we seek to understand these "drivers" so that we can begin to use them versus them using us. (Remember, understanding doesn't necessarily mean agreement.)

Them

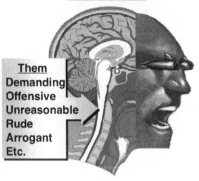

Them
Demanding
Offensive
Unreasonable
Rude
Arrogant
Etc.

If we look below the surface of a difficult person's behavior, we will first see that he/she is stuck in their brainstem, and therefore we must assume that the limbic system has engaged this part of the brain because it interpreted certain data as threatening. Further, because we now know that their interpretations are created by their beliefs and perceptions, we must also assume that this person has certain beliefs about us, himself/herself, and/or the world that is causing all of this to happen.

For example, would you imagine that this difficult person sees the world as safe or unsafe? Also, what do you suppose this person believes about the concepts of trust and cooperation? Further, given the reactive quality of his/her emotions and behaviors, what would you imagine this person thinks of themselves...high self-esteem or low?

When answering these questions about a difficult person, it's easy to see how they might see the world as unsafe (i.e. people are out to get them) and further, how these people would tend to reject the qualities of trust and cooperation as dangerous.

The trick is to not be fooled by their arrogance, or what seems to be "confidence" in the righteousness of their position. This is not a sign of high self-esteem, but of low. When someone is truly confident in who they are and what they believe, they have no need to attack others. In fact, it is because of their confidence that they can become curious about an opposing position without feeling threatened. It is actually the person who is afraid that there is something wrong with them (low self esteem) that needs to dominate others and/or prove others wrong. Thus, when someone is being argumentative, defensive, arrogant, etc., it is a clear sign of a lack of self-confidence and/or low self-esteem.

"Those that love to be feared and fear to be loved, they themselves are more frightened than anyone."
Saint Frances de Sales

Why is this important to us? Because, when we are dealing with someone who believes that the world is a dangerous place, that trust and cooperation are dangerous, and that there is something wrong with them, and we respond in old, reactive ways (i.e., we become defensive, annoyed, and argumentative), we become part of the problem. In other words, when we respond to their brainstem from our brainstem, without meaning to, our reactions will reinforce their fear-based beliefs about themselves and the world, and thus support the very behavior we want them to change!

This is why dealing with difficult people can be so...well...difficult! As we have learned, they see us as the problem, we see them as the problem, and as a result, the cycle of conflict/resistance is born and exacerbated. We now know that we can't start by trying to change them because they will only interpret this as criticism, which means that we must start by changing our beliefs about them if we want to be successful.

This, of course, is easier said than done because when someone is being arrogant, argumentative, and generally obnoxious, it's easy to see them as unacceptable, offensive, reprehensible, and just plain wrong! However, now we know that if we hold on to this belief and/or interpretation, we will not only validate their negative beliefs about us, but also engage our brainstem and limit our ability to respond in a purposeful manner.

Therefore, let's examine how we might choose

to see or define these people in a way that engages the "top of our mind" instead.

Basically, this means being willing to define "them" on purpose, or in a way that is both accurate <u>and</u> allows us to choose our reaction. Given that people who are being stubborn, defensive, argumentative, etc. must be coming from the part of their brain designed to deal with fear (their brainstem), then it would follow that we could accurately describe them as "frightened." Maybe not frightened in the traditional sense of someone recoiling out of fear, but more in terms of how we could describe the energy behind their behavior. As we look back at past interactions with difficult people, we could probably put, "They were worried or afraid that ..." in front of what they were thinking. For example, they were afraid that we thought they were wrong... we wouldn't listen...we didn't understand the seriousness of the situation...we wouldn't give them what they want, etc.

In fact, before learning about what is really going on here (how people become trapped in the brainstem), we could have also defined ourselves as coming from the worried or fear-based part of our brain as well. In other words, we were afraid that they would make us upset, they couldn't be reasoned with, they would cause more problems, make us look bad, etc.

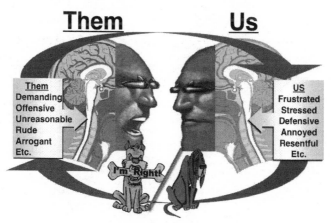

Therefore, changing how we define the problem, seeing their behavior (as well as our old reactions) as frightened versus frightening is not only more accurate, it also takes some of the threat out of how we interpret their behavior, and thus allows us to respond more purposefully.

For example, imagine that we are in a room full of friends and colleagues, and a little kid bursts in and begins telling us what horrible people we are. We wouldn't react by beginning to defend ourselves and/or telling him that he, not us is the horrible person! No, because we would see/interpret his behavior as coming from his fear (i.e., see him as frightened), we would most likely begin to ask him questions around how we could help ("Are you lost? "Where is your Mom or Dad?" In other words, based upon our ability to see him as frightened, we are then able to respond to him from the more purposeful, compassionate part of our brain.

This is exactly what I suggest we do with what, in the past, we might have described as a "difficult person"... change our description of them from difficult to frightened. Not only will this diminish our tendency to see their behavior as offensive and/or dangerous, it will also give us an opportunity to respond to them in a more purposeful manner. Plus, as I have mentioned, it's simply more accurate. When we can see how another's behavior is coming from the lower 20% of their brain, it allows for the fact that this is only 20% of who they really are.

Of course, some people are so frightened so much of the time that they almost seem to live in their brainstem. However, this is not really all of who they are. It is very possible that when they are doing something they love and/or are interacting with someone they love, that they are a very different person. Why? Because in these situations, they are coming from a very different part of their brain. There is a quote I use in my presentations on leadership that speaks to this ability to see beyond the mask of resistance that many people wear when they are upset. It says:

"True vision is seeing in another <u>more</u> than they are showing you."
Adapted from Neale Donald Walsch

Therefore, if becoming influential with others is your goal, then seeing their resistant behavior for what it is (the product of the frightened part of their brain) could serve you well in choosing a response. In fact, you could then become curious about who they are behind this mask, or who they are when they are not frightened, because it is this "other person" who is able to access their higher-order thinking and is the most capable of hearing what you have to say and responding intelligently. (More on how to motivate them to shift to this "Top of the Mind" persona later.)

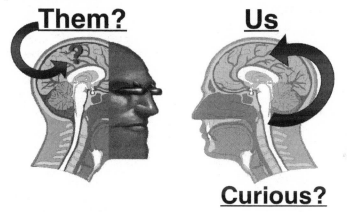

So, now we know:

- Why the cycle of conflict / resistance is so common in today's world (people are stuck in their brain stems).

- Why it is so important for us to know what we

want to practice going into these situations.

- How to regain control when we lose it (the BRAIN model).

- Why these other people seem to cling to their position. (They are frightened, worried, stressed.)

- Why we must change our beliefs about them in order to be successful with them. (Because our beliefs determine how our limbic system interprets their behavior, and thus what part of our brain is engaged as a result.)

As we apply this knowledge, the good news is that something <u>will</u> change. Why? Because we have changed our part of the interaction. We are no longer doing the same "dance," so to speak.

A noted psychologist and author by the name of Harriet Lerner has written several books on this subject and interpersonal effectiveness. The perspective that Dr. Lerner uses to describe both the problem and the solution is that the way in which we respond to others and how others respond to us can be conceptualized as a dance with very predictable steps. Just as in any learned pattern of behavior, the longer these steps are practiced, the more automatic they become. From this perspective, it's easy to see how we all have been practicing certain "steps" with those we have labeled "difficult" for quite a while.

However, as we become skilled at choosing the qualities and characteristics we want to practice, as we begin to use interactions with others as an opportunity to make a statement about who we are, and as we practice seeing others who may be upset as frightened and only showing us a small part of who they really are, we can change our "steps," which then changes the dance and forces the other to change something as well.

As Dr. Lerner suggests, this doesn't necessarily mean that these "others" will always be happy about the change. In fact, they may try to force us to return to the familiar "dance" of the past because this old pattern of behavior is familiar to them, and they may fear what they don't understand. However, if we just continue to come from our more purposeful "Top of the Mind" perspective, we can weather their attempts to influence us, and do so in such a way that we actually begin to influence them. In order to do this, however, we must be applying all aspects of the POWER model, so let's continue to see how clarity about "The Wisdom of Serenity" might support us in this endeavor.

CHAPTER *18*

Difficult People & The Wisdom of Serenity

Because we have already discussed the importance of *serenity* as a precursor to acceptance, courage, wisdom, and change earlier in Chapter Twelve, I won't repeat this information here. However, feel free to re-read this material as a prelude to applying this step to your interactions with others if you like, because it does pertain to what we are wanting to accomplish.

This third step in the POWER model addresses our tendency to try to change "them" first as a way to resolve the conflict, and our further tendency to use our negative emotions as fuel for this change process. We now know why this won't work (the Lesson of the Fist), however, the temptation may still persist.

What the "wisdom of serenity" suggests may be the hardest thing to do in dealing with others, because it states unequivocally that in order to be successful with these people, we must first accept them as they are! I know, a part of our brain is saying, "WHAT? ACCEPT THEIR BEING RUDE, AR-ROGANT, DEMANDING, AND TREATING ME WITH DISRESPECT? NEVER!!!!!!!!!!

Other than noticing which part of our brain is becoming so resistant here, there is another bit of awareness that we might want to bring to the process of becoming more effective in these situations, i.e., the reason we have so much trouble with the concept of acceptance is because we see it as condoning their behavior and/or giving up, or giving in to them. To be clear, this is not my suggestion. In fact, my goal is to help you become more influential in situations such as these. However, I still say that the way to achieve this is to begin with *acceptance*.

What I mean by the term "acceptance," has nothing to do with approval or surrender, but instead is an awareness of what is, and an ability to imagine ourselves dealing with the situation without any-thing needing to change. It means that we recognize that they are upset, and see this less as a threat, and more as "good information" about what part of their brain is engaged, and what they believe. We don't have to agree with their rationale for being upset, but we do have to acknowledge that this is the situation with which we are faced, and that trying to change them (at least for the moment) will only make the situation worse.

The reason for this is simple. Unless we can accept "what is" (they are upset), then we will be continually trapped in the part of our brain that is threatened and needs to change something outside of ourselves before we can be effective. Given that our goal is exactly the opposite (to shift from the brainstem to more of a "Top of the Mind" perspective), we must invoke the power of serenity and acceptance because both are neocortex concepts. Remember, the "Serenity Prayer" is not a plea for serenity, but a process that describes how to use this "Top of the Mind" concept to become more powerful (influential) in our lives, and in the lives of others.

The *wisdom of serenity* with people goes like this:
1. Serenity allows us to accept them as they are (for the moment), which then allows us to focus our courage and energy for change on the area over which we have the most influence... ourselves.

2. This ensures that we are coming from the "Top of the Mind" and thus, can bring all of our clarity, confidence, and creativity to bear on becoming more influential with them.

This is also why it is so important to come into these interactions clear about the wisdom/importance of serenity, or if we miss this opportunity and find ourselves reacting from our brainstem, why it's important to use the BRAIN model to regain a sense of serenity/acceptance, and then come back to these interactions with a clear picture of what we want to practice, and who we want to be. The challenge is to recognize that the neocortex concept of serenity is the precursor for all of this, meaning that we cannot be successful with others (or with anything) unless we are able to first access this quality.

The good news is that the BRAIN model is designed to create this clear "Top of the Mind" experience of serenity. The bad news is that this has not been our habitual way of dealing with conflict in the past, and thus it will not feel familiar at first. However, as mentioned earlier, just because a way of being is unfamiliar, it doesn't mean that we shouldn't make it part of who we are. In fact, given how similar the word "familiar" is to the word, "familial," and given how many of our habitual ways of dealing with conflict were born in our family, it's very possible that our reactions to others are simply carryovers from what we learned growing up. This is not an indictment of our family, just an explanation of why some ways of being feel more familiar than others.

If you have determined that your habitual

learned ways of dealing with others are not serving you (they are not producing the results you desire and are incongruent with the statement you want to make about who you are), then these first three steps (clarity of purpose, our past/P.I.E., and the wisdom of serenity) should be very helpful in crafting new responses that if practiced will eventually feel comfortable and familiar.

CHAPTER *19*

Difficult People & Our Energy
(Getting "Them" to Shift)

When I am speaking of "energy" with respect to how we deal with difficult people and conflict, I am actually referring to two separate concepts. The first is a fairly straight forward distinction between being active or receptive, and a model for how and when to use each if our goal is to become more influential with others. The second is more abstract, but is also critical to our success and is woven into the new model I am going to introduce in this chapter.

Yes, I am finally going to give you a model for how to motivate those "frightened" people (in the past we may have called them "difficult") to shift from their brainstem up into their neocortex so that you will (a) be dealing with a more rational being, (b) become more successful in drawing their best thinking into the problem-solving process, and (c) be interacting with the part of them that can actually hear your information as valuable versus threatening.

Of course, first we must ensure that we are applying all of the material presented to date. In other words, we must be clear about the qualities and characteristics we want to bring to the interaction, and we must have purposefully chosen our beliefs concerning those with whom we want to be influential (seeing them as frightened versus obnoxious). We also must be VERY aware of the wisdom of serenity, or the importance of accepting the fact that they are upset, not as the problem, but as good information about where to begin.

Next, we must choose whether to be active or receptive in terms of how we engage these individuals or groups. This is important because, in order for any communication to go forward in a productive way, one person must be active and the other receptive. Unfortunately, most of us have been taught that the active role is the most powerful. Why? Because as children we experienced our parents and teachers actively telling us what to do while we were supposed to be receptive and listen to their directions.

This taught us that powerful people are active and do the talking, while the less powerful (or even powerless) are supposed to be receptive, and thus we resist this "receptive" position today because it seems less powerful, or influential.

However, let's look at what is going on when we are dealing with someone who is upset. Do you think this (upset) person is more likely to be active or receptive? Most would agree that these people are actively resisting what we have to say, and/or trying to convince us of something, and thus could accurately be described as being more active than receptive. So, what happens when they are active, and we respond by actively defending our position and/or trying to convince them to change? You guessed it, the "Lesson of the Fist" becomes the order of the day and the cycle of resistance/frustration is born and exacerbated.

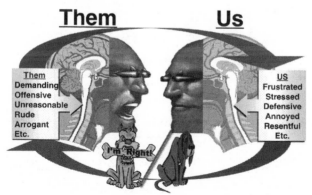

Therefore, while at some point we do want to be able to bring our ideas into the conversation and have them heard as valuable information, to do this too soon will almost guarantee failure. Even if we are being "appropriately active," i.e., presenting our views in a calm, rational manner, if they are actively resisting or defending their own perspective, they will not hear what we have to say.

Of course, this is not to say that all people are like this. There may well be many people that come to you with a problem, you take the active role and give them your solution and they say, "Thanks!". In this case, the active role is very effective because the person is being receptive to your ideas and/or directions. The problem lies with those people who in the past we might have labeled as "difficult," and who we now know to be simply stuck in the lower 20% of their brain. Because these people are being actively resistant, we must begin by being receptive if our goal is to become more influential.

When I suggest a receptive position with regard to these frightened individuals, however, I am not just talking about becoming passive while they rant and rave. Neither am I suggesting that we just let them "vent" until they have "gotten it all out," and then tell them what we want them to know. Instead, I suggest that we become very curious (a receptive, neocortex quality) about what is driving their thoughts and emotions so that we can eventually turn this information from the problem to part of the solution, and motivate them to shift to the upper 80% of their brain.

To accomplish, this I suggest we revisit a quote I introduced earlier in Chapter Thirteen:

"Stress is an indicator of our belief in the value and validity of our worries and fears."
Bill Crawford

It's easy to see that people who are upset are certainly "stressed" in some way. If we follow the logic of this last quote, we can see that this "stress" is an indicator that they are holding on to certain fear-based beliefs...beliefs about themselves (powerless/flawed) and the world (threatening/unsafe) that are being driven by the energies of worry and fear.(They are afraid that . . . or worried that . . .). There are several potential areas of worry and fear that could be driving their behavior, however, the overriding fear of most people who are upset is that they are going to be criticized or somehow blamed for the problem.

Part of this concern may very well stem from their awareness that indeed, they may be responsible for the problem in some way. (They didn't keep their word, meet a deadline, keep an agreement, etc.) However, because this fear is tied to their self esteem, they will be even less likely to hear your solution, especially if you forget the main rule in dealing with conflict. I call this the "You Stupid Idiot" rule, and it may be one of the most important concepts to keep in mind when dealing with people who are upset.

The "You Stupid Idiot" Rule:

You should never talk to anyone in such a way that they could put "You stupid idiot" on the end of anything you say!

For example, when a classmate keeps making the same mistake over and over, you might become frustrated and say: *"George! How many times do I have to tell you? You just can't keep screwing this up!"* (and under your breath you say or at least think: *"You stupid idiot"*) Or, with a friend who disagrees with you on a certain subject, you might find yourself saying, *"No, you're not listening to me, in fact, you never listen to me."* (...you stupid idiot)." Or with a family member that is questioning your choice of majors, you might be tempted to say, *"Don't you understand? This is what I love to do! I don't want to have a fall-back career!"* (...you stupid idiot)."

I know, some of you may be thinking, "Oh my goodness, I won't be able to talk for the next three months," because when we are dealing with someone who is being dismissive, rude, and ignoring the facts, it's so easy to think of them as a stupid idiot! However, if we do, meaning if we speak to them in such a way that they can put "You stupid idiot" on the end of our sentences, they will put it on there whether we say it or not, and drive them deeper into their "resistant brain."

This was brought home to me very clearly by my son, Chris who came to me when he was in high school with an unusual request. He and his classmates were doing reports on what their parents did for a living, and so he came to me with this puzzled look on his face and asked, *"Okay, Dad, what is it that you do again?"* (You know, being a psychologist is a hard thing to describe sometimes.) I responded in what I thought was a succinct and even brilliant manner by saying, *"Well, Christopher, I help people with their happiness!"*

He laughed and said, *"No, Dad, trust me, I can't go and tell my classmates that...what do you really do?"* I began to describe how I give seminars and see individuals in counseling, but he interrupted and said, *"No, Dad, I need a concrete example of what you actually tell people in your role as a psychologist."* I said, "Okay, I tell people about the 'You Stupid Idiot' Rule." He looked at me quizzically and said, *"The You Stupid Idiot Rule... what's that?"* I said, *"Well, I believe that whenever you are talking to someone, you should never speak to them in such a way that they could put 'you stupid idiot' on the end of the sentence."* His

243

eyes brightened, and he said, *"Oh really?"* and turned around and walked off. I thought, oh well, he must have gotten all the information he needed, and thus didn't give it another thought.

About two weeks later, we were having a problem with some chore he had "forgotten" to do for the umpteenth time, and I must have gone into my brainstem, because I was saying something like, *"Christopher, how many times have I told you that. . ."* at which point, he interrupted me and with a little mischievous smile said: *"Uh, Dad, have you forgotten the 'you stupid idiot' rule?"*

Ouch! He was right. I was speaking to him in a way that he could very easily put, "you stupid idiot" on the end of my sentences. At that point, to my credit, I was able to resist the temptation to berate him even further for catching me not practicing what I preached, and instead said: *"Christopher, you're right. Clearly, I'm upset right now, and while this wasn't the best way to talk about it, we do have a problem here. Why don't I take a moment to calm down, and we can discuss how to solve this problem."*

You see, I would never want Christopher to think that I saw him as a "stupid idiot." However, it was true that I was speaking to him in a way that he could have easily put "you stupid idiot" on the end of my statement, and thus without meaning to, I was working against both of our best interests. I tell you this story to illustrate how easy it is for us to fall into this trap, and to encourage you to be very aware of how we are engaging those with whom we want to be influential. Because, if they sense we are being critical of them, or blaming them for the problem in any way, they will react by becoming more upset, and thus becoming more the way we don't want them to be.

To be clear, I'm not just talking about tone of voice here, I am referring to all of the nonverbals (body language, facial expression, etc.) that influence how someone interprets what we are telling them. However, rather than becoming worried and/or stressed about whether our brows are knitted or our arms are crossed in a "closed" position, all we really have to do is follow the first three steps in this model.

In other words, if we have chosen the qualities we want to practice and changed our beliefs about the person who is upset so that we see them as frightened versus difficult, and accessed the "wisdom of serenity" which allows us to accept them as they are (at least for the moment), this will go a long way toward helping us interact with them in a successful way, or at least in a manner that doesn't imply that we think they are a "stupid idiot."

Of course, in addition to being aware of "how" we interact with them, there is the factor of "when" to offer a solution as well. Even if we are speaking to them in a respectful way, if we try to make them change their beliefs, or change their position too soon, we will again only motivate them to tighten their fist and resist us even more. Therefore, given that it is clear that they are stressed and worried about something, I suggest that we begin by harnessing or working with that energy versus against it. In other words, if we can discover what is driving their resistance, we will be in a much better position to harness that driver and reverse the direction of the information.

To accomplish this, I am going to identify four of these drivers, or four ways their stress, worry, or fear might block their ability to engage in successful problem-solving, and how we might effectively respond to each.

Block/Driver # 1: They are, of course, very invested in the righteousness of their position, and very motivated to convince us that they are right. Their fear is that we won't listen, and that anything we say will be an effort to convince them that they are wrong. (This is why attempting to problem-solve or even get your point of view across at this point is fruitless, even if your solution is a good one.)
Suggestion: Listen and learn. Listen, not to placate them or "just let them vent," but to discover (learn) the key to their cooperation. In other words, what is the belief/interpretation that is driving their brainstem reaction? Holding these questions in your mind should be helpful: What are they concerned or worried about? What do they want you to know? What

is most important to them as an outcome? The best way to discover these keys is to listen to what they are saying without needing to counter their logic or their position. If they are so frightened that they are not making any sense, you can ask them questions about this key, such as:

• What are you most concerned about here?
• What do you want me to know about this situation? and/or
• What is most important to you here?

The important thing to remember is that you are gathering data about what is driving their brainstem reaction, not engaging in a debate about who's right. I would also suggest that you listen in a way that will allow you to paraphrase what you hear, if necessary. Of course, listening and paraphrasing are pretty standard communication tools, however, I am suggesting that you use them in different ways than most books on conflict resolution. For example, I am not suggesting that you listen and paraphrase simply to allow the other person to feel "understood." In fact, my guess is that when most people are dealing with someone who is being arrogant and/or rude, at that moment they could care less as to whether this person feels "understood." Instead, I'm suggesting that you draw your motivation to listen from your desire to discover their driver or key, so that you can harness that energy, and at some point become more influential in the interaction.

In addition, I'm not even suggesting that you need to paraphrase everything you hear, especially if this comes in the form of just repeating what they say. For example, when someone tells you that they are feeling angry and frustrated, I am not suggesting that you then say, "I hear you are feeling angry and frustrated!" Chances are they will interpret this as some technique you read in a book, and will very likely become even more angry and frustrated as a result. I am suggesting that you listen so that you could paraphrase if necessary. This is a very different form of listening than most of us practice, especially in an argument. Listening so that you could paraphrase is closer to how we listen to directions when getting to some destination as soon as possible is our priority.

For example, let's assume that we are lost on a country road, and we are trying to get to a lake house where our friends and family are waiting on us for dinner. We stop a local and ask directions, and he says: "The old Crawford place? Sure, I know where that is. You just go on down this road until you see a big tree on your right. Then you turn left and go, say, about a mile or two until you see a pond on your left, and turn right. You then keep on going until the road goes over a big hill, and you will come to a fork in the road and that's where you turn left. After that, you just look for a grove of trees with a house in the middle, and that's the place. You can't miss it!"

Hmmmmm? At this point, because this is very valuable information and we want to make sure we heard it correctly, we might say, "Okay, let me get this straight. You go down this road . . ." In other words, we would paraphrase what we heard to check for accuracy, because if we don't get it right, we won't be able to get to where we want to go.

This is exactly how and why we want to listen to the frightened person with whom we may be having a conversation. What they are telling us is very valuable information about where they are, and this information will be critical to our getting where we want to go with them, i.e., motivating them to shift to the more rational part of their brain and willingly participating in the problem-solving process.

Plus, if you remember, one of their concerns is that we won't listen, and thus they may challenge us at some point by saying something like: "You haven't heard a word I have said, have you?!!" If we have been listening in this very specific way, we can say, "Well, what I have heard so far is _____." And then, we ask two magic questions, first: "Is there anything else?" and eventually, "Did I get it right?"

Often, what is really bothering people is not what they are complaining about, but something deeper. If we are willing to continue asking, "Is there anything else?" (in a caring and interested tone, of course), they will either eventually tell us what is really bothering them, or confirm that what they have told us is indeed the real issue. Then when we paraphrase what we heard to ensure we understood them correctly and ask, "Did I get it right?" we once again confirm our desire to understand and give ourselves the opportunity to see if there was anything we missed.

I mean, how many times has someone thought they knew what you were thinking, *but they were wrong?!!*

Given that this experience is very common for most people, isn't it fair to say that if misunderstanding happens <u>to</u> us (we are misunderstood by others), that it also happens <u>from</u> us (we may be misunderstanding others)? If so, we want to ensure that we get it all and get it right if we want to be in the powerful position of crafting a solution that they can hear and support.

In addition, there is another reason to listen in such a way that you can paraphrase. It's very common for people who are stuck in their brainstem to go off on rants and tangents that seem to have no real connection to the original problem. They may say one or two things that are meaningful, and then go off into the wild blue yonder on some third issue that no one can do anything about. If you are listening so that you can paraphrase, this is your opportunity to interrupt them and redirect the conversation in the only way they will allow. For example, if they sense that you are wanting to interrupt them to counter their position, they will very likely resist. You can say, "But, but, but..." all day long, trying to get a word in edgewise, and they will try just as hard to keep on talking, because the word, "but" signals that you are wanting to counter what they just said.

However, if you say something like, "Okay, let me make sure I'm getting this right ...," or even, "I don't want to forget what you said earlier. Could you tell me more about ...," they are going to be much more willing to let you interrupt them because they are invested in you getting it right. Plus, at this point, you can paraphrase what you heard them say on the first two pertinent points (leaving out the tangent), and ask them to tell you more about these issues. You will be amazed at how this refocuses the conversation on the more germane information, and moves the process along at the same time.

Block/Driver # 2: They are afraid that we don't understand the seriousness of the problem, or that we believe they shouldn't be (or have no valid reason to be) so upset. They not only believe that their problem is serious, they believe that they have a right to be upset about it. In fact, they may even interpret your not being upset as you don't think their problem is a big deal, or that you just don't care.

Remember when we discussed the folly of trying to get someone to just calm down, they generally don't say, "What a wonderful idea. Calm down, I never thought of that. Thank you for sharing." In fact, they will probably say something like, "Calm down? Don't tell me to calm down!," and become even more upset.

The reason for this is that these people are stuck in the brainstem and this part of the brain doesn't want to listen or calm down. In fact, the brainstem interprets listening as powerless... if you are talking and I'm listening, you have won and I have lost. So, what can we do? How can we respond in a way that allows them to stop defending the seriousness of their problem, and their right to be upset?

Suggestion: Empathize: I know, this can sound like psychobabble, so let me explain. By "empathize," I don't mean that you need to "feel their pain," hold their hand, or become their counselor. In fact, this step, while essential, takes only a few seconds, and could be accomplished as easily as saying something like, "I can see how you would be upset by this."

Many people have trouble with this concept because they are afraid that in order to empathize with someone's position (or why they might be upset), they must agree with them. The important thing to remember here is that;

Understanding doesn't necessarily mean agreement!

It just means that given what we now know about how negative beliefs can drive someone into their brainstem, we can see how they might be upset. For example, imagine you are dealing with a person who is angry because he believes that he has been treated unfairly in some way. If you were to say, "I don't know where you are getting this. You are being treated just like everyone else!," he would most likely become even more angry, and redouble his efforts to defend his position. If, on the other hand, you said something like, "Hmmmmm, I can see how you would be upset by that," it wouldn't mean that you agreed with him. It would, however, allow him to give up the need to defend his position, or his right to believe what he believes, and thus he would be more open to what you have to say next. This leads us to the third block to effective communication, and yet another driver of their brainstem reaction.

Block/Driver # 3: They are afraid that we either don't value their opinion, or that we are going to continue to argue for the fact that we are right and they are wrong. This concern is understandable because, in the past, I'm sure that most of the people with whom they have disagreed have indeed argued with them about who's right. However, this is also where we can become more influential in that we are not going to respond like "most people." In fact, now that we have information about what is important to them (gathered in Step One: Listen/learn), and have used Step Two (empathize) to defuse their need to defend their position, we can now begin to encourage them then to shift from their brainstem up into their neocortex. This is accomplished by asking "Top of the Mind," or neocortex questions, versus brainstem questions.

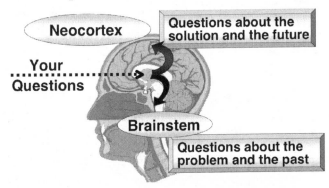

Brainstem questions are generally about the past and the problem, and are heard by most people as an attempt to identify "who's wrong." They can include, but are not limited to: "Why did you do that? What do you expect me to do about it? Where did you get that idea? What were you thinking? How many times do I have to tell you . . .?" etc. These types of questions will also almost always violate the "You Stupid Idiot rule," meaning that one could easily put "You Stupid Idiot" on the end of the phrase, and this increases the likelihood that the person you are attempting to influence will be driven further into their brainstem, and become even more resistant.

Given that the brainstem is not where you want them to be, I suggest that you instead ask "neocortex questions" which are questions about the future and the solution. These will differ slightly depending on the type of conflict you are dealing with. For example, if you are dealing with a classmate, this could be as simple as asking, "What do you see as a solution here?" or "How would you suggest we resolve this?"

Unfortunately, many people are afraid to ask these sorts of questions because they are worried that the person will ask for something they can't deliver. However, I suggest that even if this is the case, asking this question is a very important step because it moves the focus of the discussion from the past and "who's to blame," to a discussion about the future and a solution. Almost every discussion involving conflict is about *who* did *what* in the past. Unfortunately, this will be a fruitless debate, because they will remember it one way while you will remember it another, and both of you will be trying to prove the other wrong. Therefore, one benefit of asking a question about what they want in the future is that at least we are now discussing what will *be*, versus what *was*, and the discussion is no longer about "who's to blame."

The second reason for asking the, "What do you see as a solution?" question is that it gives you even more information about what is important to them, and thus more information about the key to their cooperation. Sometimes, people (especially stressed-out classmates or family members) seem to think that in order to get anyone to pay attention to them, they must be upset (the "squeaky wheel" syndrome). Therefore, they may act very upset when what they are wanting is actually no big deal. By asking, we know exactly what we are dealing with, and we might find that we can accommodate them much easier than we first thought.

On the other hand, if the person with whom you are dealing is a friend or family member (or anyone else whom you have known for a while), and they are accusing you of something you didn't do, you can apply the neocortex concept here as well. After first listening (without defending yourself), you can move directly to asking "Top of the Mind" questions, stating, "Hmmmmm, is that really congruent with (does this really fit with) who you know me to be?" Most people will be caught a bit off guard by the question, which is good because it means that this has interrupted their brainstem thinking, and thus created an opportunity for them to shift up to the "top of their mind." This will also have them thinking twice about accusing you unjustly in the future, because they know they will be asked this question.

Of course, if they respond to the question, "Is this congruent with who you know me to be?" with

"Yes, it is!," then a second neocortex question might be in order, such as, "Really? What have you seen me do that would give you the impression I am that kind of person?" If they then describe a situation where they misinterpreted your behavior or intent, you can say, "Oh that makes sense, would you like to know what I was really thinking?" All this should have them reassessing their criteria for accusing you, and again should affect whether they continue to do this in the future. What is important, however, is to note that in none of these cases did we defend ourselves, or match their brainstem energy with our own.

Of course, if you are dealing with a younger sibling or someone you are mentoring, you will want to approach the conversation differently. Usually in these situations, the mentee has made some mistake, and you are wanting them to correct the situation and avoid this sort of problematic behavior in the future. Unfortunately, most people try to accomplish this by focusing on the mistake and the problems it caused. While this is understandable, this tact is rarely successful because this emphasis on the pain of the problem will only drive the younger person deeper into their brainstem, and thus limit their ability to bring their best thinking to the learning process.

Given that our goal is to ensure that they shift to the "top of their mind," we can begin by listening to their side of the story without the need to either agree or argue. This will take a lot of skill and patience, however, it is a critical component of success because (a) they are probably afraid that we won't listen, and (b) by listening, we can learn what they are concerned about, and/or what is important to them (the key to their cooperation).

Even if what we hear is some story about how they are not to blame, this can become very important information because it gives us a place to start. In other words,

In order to influence someone, we must start where they are!

Or, put another way . . .

If our goal is to motivate others, we must begin with what is motivating them!

This means our starting point must be the part of their brain (and the belief, interpretation, or concern) that is driving their emotions and behavior. When someone is becoming defensive about who's to blame, this indicates that they are being driven by their desire to avoid being seen in a negative light. This is good information because it allows us to partner with this desire (empathize), and ask a question about the future versus trying to force them to admit to and / or feel bad about what they have done in the past.

In other words, rather than argue with them about whether they are to blame, we can empathize with their desire to be seen in a positive light (a neocortex concept) by following their declaration of innocence with, "Yes, I can see how you would be upset by this, and that you really want to find a solution here."

As you might imagine, few people would argue with this statement, and thus we now have switched the discussion to the importance of success in the future versus avoidance of blame. Given that a solution is something we want as well, we can follow their agreement with something like, "Good. I've got some ideas about how I can help you with this.

Now the focus can be on what was learned, and their ability to influence how they are perceived by others. Once they have agreed to your helping them succeed, you can continue in this vein and have them reexamine their mistake by saying something like, "Okay, let me make sure I'm not telling you something you already know. Given what you know now, how would you do this differently in the future?"

This question has them rethinking their behavior from more of a "Top of the Mind" perspective versus "who's to blame." If they have trouble coming up with a response, you can give them another way of looking at the problem by asking, "If you were teaching someone to do this in a way that would have the most potential for success, what would you suggest that they do?" Of course, you might choose different words here, but the specific words aren't important. What is important is that you are engaging them in a way that minimizes conflict (as well as the potential of their going into shame or blame), and maximizes their desire to find a solution.

As you can see, listening, empathizing, and asking neocortex questions are critical steps in dealing with people when they are upset. What you may or may not have noticed, however, is that all of these steps are receptive in nature. This is what I mean when I say that when dealing with conflict, it is the receptive position that is initially the most powerful.

Plus, these steps change the color of the interaction in a way that makes the last step, problem-solving, more successful. In other words, our willingness to practice these receptive skills will not only give us valuable information about the key to their cooperation and allow them to shift from their brainstem to their neocortex, it will gradually reduce the "us versus them" nature of the conflict, and allow them to see us less as an adversary, and more as an ally.

Of course, at some point, we are going to want to take an active position if our goal is to be influential with this person. I just want to caution against going to the active step of problem-solving too soon, i.e., before you know the key to their cooperation, and/or before they have shifted from the brainstem to the neocortex.

How will you know if it's too soon? They will balk at your solution. This could come in the form of a "Yes, but ...," or "I tried that and it didn't work," or some other statement that lets us know that the real key to their cooperation, or what's really important to them, is missing in the solution we offered. If this happens, the challenge will be to see this response as "good information" (versus a problem that will engage our brainstem), and repeat steps 1-3 to determine what we missed.

Of course, in the best-case scenario, when we ask a neocortex question, they will give us a solution we can support, and we just go with it. I say "best-case," because when the solution comes from them, it will automatically contain the key to their cooperation, and thus they will be much more likely to support its implementation. At this point, the problem-solving stage is simply about confirming logistics and moving forward with a mutually agreed upon plan of action.

What is more likely, however, is that we will need to bring all that we learned from the first three steps into the problem-solving stage, and blend this information (what's important to them and what's important to us) in a very purposeful manner. This might sound something like, "Okay, I know that (fill in the blank with what you learned in step one and three) is important to you, so I suggest (insert your "blended" solution here). Would you be willing to give this a try?"

There are two important components of this problem-solving statement that are worth noting:

1. It begins with our conceptualization of what's important to them. This not only assures them that we heard them correctly, it gives them reason to be optimistic that at least some of this is being incorporated into the solution.

2. The solution isn't framed as a "take it or leave it" proposition, but instead as something that is worth trying. This is almost always the best way to suggest a solution because it helps the person(s) we are wanting to influence feel more comfortable with the idea, because they know that if it doesn't work, there will be an opportunity to revisit the decision. People will almost always be more willing to "try" something rather than be forced to either accept or reject a proposal out of hand.

Of course, before you even move to the problem-solving phase of this process, you must decide whether this is the best time to offer a solution.

Often, people are so invested in their position and trapped in their brainstem (angry, frustrated, etc.) that they are not open to anything. When this is the case, postponing the problem-solving phase of the discussion often has the effect of allowing them to calm down and think about the questions you have asked. In addition, it can also give you time to think about how you are going to frame the solution, or how you are going to blend their key with yours.

The good news is that you have listened to them and learned what is important to them and what they are concerned about (the key to their co-operation). You have empathized with them so that they no longer need to defend their right to be upset, and you have asked them neocortex questions about their ideas, which gives them the opportunity to shift to the "Top of their Mind" as they think about the future and what they want to accomplish, versus the past and who's to blame. If you have determined that postponing the discussion and giving everyone time to think about the solution is the best idea, the challenge will be to do so in a way that they will hear it as good information.

One final tip... remember to use the magic word "and" versus "but" as a transition from the receptive position to the active. Many people have learned that it's a good idea to acknowledge what another says before they offer their own opinion. Unfortunately, when this is done using the word "but" as the transition, it will likely fail, because "but" negates whatever comes before it.

For example, imagine during a disagreement someone says this to you, "Yeah, I hear what you're saying, BUT . . ." Chances are that you will not be eager to hear what comes next because your position was negated with the word "but." It's like going up to a member of your family and saying, "I really love you, BUT . . ." The words "I really love you" are immediately negated by the word "but," and thus the person with whom you are wanting to communicate will not be inclined to be open to what you have to say next.

Instead, use the word "and." For example, "I hear what you are saying *and* I have some ideas about the situation as well." This allows people to be more open to what you are about to say because you have not negated what they just said. In fact, you have set up a situation where you can draw from what they think/believe/want, and what is important to you in crafting a solution. This increases the potential that your solution will be heard in a positive light because you have included something that's important to them.

This is especially true when you are wanting to correct someone's behavior. In fact, thinking of "correcting" this person's behavior in terms of, "How can my solution be valuable in helping them get what they want?" is an excellent way to conceptualize how you might want to frame your suggestion for change. Or, put another way:

The most effective form of correction is when the other feels informed versus chastised.

As you may have noticed, this most recent model which is designed to help resistant individuals shift from their brainstem to their neocortex spells LEAP (*Listen/Learn, Empathize, Ask* - neocortex questions, and *Problem-solve*). As I have mentioned earlier, I like my models to spell something and, whenever possible, for that word to have some meaning in terms of application. In this case, I call this the LEAP model because I believe it will take a LEAP of faith for us to practice these steps when dealing with conflict. The reason for this is that few, if any of us, grew up dealing with conflict in this way. For example, think back to when you were a child and there was a conflict in your family. How many times do you remember your parents turning to you and asking "Why dear, what are your thoughts about a solution here?" As before, this isn't meant as an indictment of our parents or our past, just good information on why this style of communication seems so unfamiliar.

Therefore, I encourage you to give yourself some time to become comfortable with the process, and also to use the power of your imagination to see yourself going through the steps with people in your mind before you try it in person. In fact, starting with less intense interactions and working your way up to those individuals who have been especially problematic in the past would be a very good idea.

Of course, I do know that there are people who are so frightened that we can LEAP with them all day long and it won't make any difference. However, I suggest that even with these people, the LEAP model is the best way to respond if your goal is to maximize success. Why? Well, for one thing, the LEAP model doesn't give them anything negative to complain about.

The interesting thing about "difficult people" is that if we were to ask them who are the difficult people in their lives, they would say us! They see our reaction as the problem, and even use this reaction to justify continuing, or even intensifying their original resistant behavior. When we are able to react by listening/learning, empathizing, asking, and then problem-solving (remembering the "You Stupid Idiot!" rule), we don't give them any "ammunition" to fire back at us or complain about. What are they going to say... "They just listened to me too much?," or "They were too interested in what I had to say?"

So, even if the person we are dealing with refuses to cooperate no matter how much we listen, empathize, etc., the fact that we have responded purposefully can serve us in that we have kept our cool, and in a way we would teach or recommend to someone we love. Plus, our ability to choose our response and define who we are, regardless of the situation, reinforces the fact that no one has the power to make us feel bad or force us to react in a negative way, even if they resist our attempts to influence the interaction.

In fact, for those of you who have taken the time to list the qualities and characteristics you want to practice when dealing with resistant individuals or groups, you should find that the LEAP model is very congruent with this vision. For example, if "patient, confident, and flexible" are representative of the "Top of the Mind" qualities you have chosen as how you want to define yourself, the willingness to first *listen* with genuine curiosity, *empathize, ask* neocortex questions, and then *problem-solve* is a behavioral model designed to bring those qualities to life.

Put another way, this is how patient, confident, and flexible people interact with the world. Thus, like the BRAIN model, the LEAP model should be helpful to those of you wanting a more tangible, concrete way to make these qualities a part of your self-definition.

Speaking of the BRAIN model, for those of you who have found this behavioral model helpful, you can certainly apply it to dealing with resistant individuals as well. For example, when we are willing to take the time to breathe, rid ourselves of tension, and ask ourselves neocortex questions (such as, how do I want to define myself at this moment, or what would I teach to someone I love?) and then imagine ourselves being this way with these people, we will also be in the best position to motivate them to shift to the "Top of their Mind" so that we can all move into productive problem-solving in a more purposeful way. This may be challenging in the heat of the moment, however, so do remember that there will be times when we just need to disengage from a particularly intense interaction, and go somewhere and use the BRAIN model to change the chemical makeup of our body, as well as shift to the "Top of our Mind." Once we have accomplished this, we will then be in an excellent position to go back into the interaction and proceed in a way that has a much higher potential for success.

Okay, so far we have discussed the cycle of conflict, or how simple disagreements can escalate into a self-perpetuating cycle, and we have learned that when we attempt to solve the problem by trying to change "the other" first, they become even more resistant (the Lesson of the Fist).

We also have discovered how their piece of the P.I.E (their beliefs about themselves, the world, and us), as well as our piece of the P.I.E. (our beliefs about them) can have a powerful effect on their behavior and on our ability to solve the problem. Further, we have examined the many reasons (stress, worry, fear) why people may be resistant in the first place, and learned a model (LEAP) that not only deals with each reason, but increases the likelihood that they will hear our suggestions in a more favorable light.

Of course, we can always use "The Four Criteria" to increase our awareness of how we want to interact with others. For example we can ask ourselves, if we were dealing with this person:

1. On purpose or deliberately . . .

2. In a way that works for us or has the effect we wanted . . .

3. In a way that makes a purposeful statement about who we are . . .

And finally,

4. In a way that we would teach to someone we love, what would this look like?

Regardless of how we do it, all of this flows from dealing with people with an awareness of our higher purpose, as well as making a decision to first employ the receptive energies of curiosity and empathy, and then shifting to the active energy of purposeful engagement/problem-solving.

Rather than trying to change them, we are instead, tying what they want with what we want, and then creating concrete agreements that bring out the best in them and support the best for all concerned.

CHAPTER 20

Difficult People & Responsibility

As mentioned earlier, the last step in the POWER model revolves around the concept of *responsibility*, and with resistant individuals, this concept must be interpreted very purposefully in order to be successful. For example, if we define "responsibility" the way most people do (i.e., "Who's responsible?" or "Who's to blame and thus should change?"), we will be thrown into the brainstem, which will limit our ability to respond. However, if we are willing to ask more purposeful questions around this concept such as, "Who do I want in control of my ability to respond?" or, "If I were taking 100% responsibility for the quality of my responses, what would they look like?" then we can easily and effectively incorporate the concept of responsibility into our model for becoming more influential or more powerful in our lives, and in the lives of others.

In order to do this responsibly, however, we must approach our interactions with others with genuineness and sincerity. In other words, my goal in presenting these models is not to turn you into a "LEAPing robot" where you are artificially "listening," and then "empathizing" and "asking" as if you are following some script. If a resistant person (or anybody, for that matter), senses that you are using some "technique" on them, they will very likely resist you even more.

You must be genuine, which means being who you are, with your own personality and unique style of communication, versus trying to "fake" some way of interacting with people that is false or phony. I am also suggesting that you choose and emphasize the aspects of your personality that are congruent with your highest purpose. The result of this "Top of the Mind" genuineness, therefore, is you at your best, or you at your most "purposeful," which I believe also equates to you at your most "powerful."

Further, you must be sincere, meaning that you must be truly invested in reaching a solution that works for everybody. The reason I am suggesting that you must sincerely pursue a mutually-beneficial solution is that when we create outcomes where either we lose or "they" lose, I believe that everybody loses.

While lawyers might be able to argue against each other in court and then go have a drink afterwards, most people will tell you that the residue left from a win/lose encounter is counterproductive to any successful collaboration in the future. Add in the stress associated with this type of confrontation, as well as the potential that the "losing party" will go and spread negative comments about you, and you have all the rationale you need to sincerely pursue a win/win solution.

In addition to being genuine and sincere, there is another distinction we must make in order to apply the L.E.A.P. and P.O.W.E.R. models successfully. We must know the difference between "influence" and "manipulation." Often when I am presenting this material, one of the participants will ask, "Isn't this just another form of manipulation?" While I can understand the confusion, I am always just a little concerned by this question, because I know that if a participant leaves the seminar wanting to be more successful in their interpersonal interactions and yet, thinks that the information presented can be used to manipulate others, he or she will be doomed to failure.

Therefore, to ensure that I don't do you the disservice of leaving you with the impression that "influence" and "manipulation" are interchangeable, let's look at how the dictionary defines these concepts:

• *"Manipulation: to control or play upon by artful, unfair, or insidious means, especially to one's own advantage."*

• *"Influence: to affect or alter by indirect or intangible means; to act upon (as a person or a person's mind or feelings) so as to effect a response."*

Can you see the difference? The definition of "manipulation" contains the words "unfair, insidious" and "to one's own advantage," while the definition of "influence" just speaks to the concept of effecting a response. This is a good example of how the energy we choose to guide our thoughts and behavior can have such a powerful effect on the results of an interaction. Bottom line, when we are attempting to manipulate someone into doing what we want, they will sense this and resist us even more. On the other hand, if our desire is instead merely to influence, and the other can see that the outcome we are trying to create is beneficial for them as well as for us, they are more likely to cooperate.

Further, they are also more likely to see subsequent interactions with us in the same light, which increases the potential for more successful outcomes in the future. That's why I'm suggesting that the

L.E.A.P. and P.O.W.E.R. models be combined so that we are drawing upon the concepts that we believe will be the most productive and beneficial for all concerned, not just practicing some "manipulative technique."

Okay, let's summarize what we have learned so far.

• First, one of the problems in dealing with "difficult" people is that their behavior has (in the past) triggered a response on our part that not only didn't help, but actually motivated them to become even more resistant. This, of course, triggered another response in us and the cycle of conflict/resistance was born and exacerbated.

• We now know that their "difficult" behavior is being generated by their brainstem, and thus when we respond in kind, everyone is coming from the lower 20 % of their brains.

• In order for us to break the cycle and become more influential in our own lives, as well as with others, we must either start from the neocortex or use the BRAIN model to shift to the "Top of our Mind," and use the situation versus the situation using us. This means we must know the qualities and/or characteristics that we want to use to define ourselves in this situation, and be willing to practice this "higher purpose" perspective as we interact with others.

• This will only be possible when we understand

how their beliefs about us and our (old) beliefs about them are driving the negative interaction. Once we understand these drivers, we can then shift from our brainstem where we saw them as obnoxious, annoying, or even frightening (intimidating), to our neocortex where we see them instead as frightened. We are then in a position to access our curiosity, and learn what's behind their mask of resistance.

In fact, this is a good time to talk about the words we use to describe others. While seeing people as annoying, intimidating, frustrating, etc. is understandable, I suggest we choose different words. Why? Because, when gerunds or words ending in "ing" are used as adjectives, they describe another's effect on us.

When that effect is positive, or congruent with our highest purpose (inspiring, motivating, etc.), then all is well. However, given that we don't want to give others the power to annoy us, intimidate us, or frustrate us, I suggest we avoid describing them as if they can.

Now back to our review.

• Having recognized that we can't be successful with people like this by trying to change them first (You should never tie your peace of mind to another's state of mind), we can now employ the *wisdom of serenity* in order to accept that they are upset. Next, we summon the courage necessary to change what we can, which initially are the qualities we are bringing to the interaction. This means that we must initially be willing to practice our highest purpose in the face of their difficult behavior so that we can bring our best to the encounter, and begin to influence them to whatever degree is possible.

• This will require our willingness to be receptive before we become active, and listen to them in order to learn *the key to their cooperation,* or what is important to them. Once we have this valuable key, we must also empathize with them so that they no longer feel that they must convince us of their right to be upset. Remember, this doesn't necessarily mean we agree with them.

• Once they are clear that they no longer need to convince us of the righteousness of their position, we can begin to ask them neocortex questions (questions about the future and the solution versus the problem and the past), which should give them the opportunity to shift from their resistant brain to their receptive brain.

• In order to accomplish this, however, we must be willing to make problem-solving the LAST thing we do in dealing with others, and ensure that we are bringing all we learned about the key to their cooperation to this final step. This means continuing to blend what is important to them with what is important to us until we come up with a solution

277

that works for everyone.

• Finally, we must *take personal responsibility for our ability to respond*, regardless of how they are with us. When we are able to do these things, we will become more influential or powerful in terms of who we are and how we feel, how they see us, and finally, how they respond to us and our message.

Of course, it isn't necessary that we limit this way of interacting with others to "difficult people." The LEAP model combined with a sense of purposeful awareness (the POWER Model) is also an excellent method of communication in general. For example:

• How valuable would it be if everyone listened to each other, and fully understood what is being said before responding?
• How valuable would it be if everyone ensured that they were coming from the most productive, intelligent part of who they are in our interactions?
• What sort of misunderstandings could be avoided if everyone checked out their beliefs and assumptions before responding?
• How valuable would it be if everyone knew that everything they said and did made a statement about who they are, and thus used their interactions with others as an opportunity to define themselves in a way that they would teach to those they love?
• To what degree would you like "neocortex," or

"Top of the Mind" questions to be the energy that drives the problem-solving efforts in your group of friends?

• How valuable would it be if everyone took personal responsibility for the quality of their responses when interacting with each other?

If these questions elicit a positive response, then the next question would seem to be, "How can I bring this 'Top of the Mind' awareness and these communication skills to my interactions and / or my friends and family?" The most obvious answer is, of course, to begin practicing this way of communicating with everyone you encounter. I suggest this because "communication" always exists as a two-way street, and often the other person is reacting to us. Therefore, if we begin to practice this type of "Top of the Mind" communication, it could trigger a similar response in others.

Of course, just being a certain way with others doesn't guarantee that everyone will follow suit. Indeed, given that few of us grew up with this "Top of the Mind" perspective as a model for success, some people may be suspicious at first. They may be afraid that this is just a trick designed to manipulate them into doing our bidding, and thus approach this new perspective with caution.

This is understandable, and therefore it will be important that we continue to practice this more purposeful way of being until others see that it's not just a superficial mask, but a profound statement about what we believe to be important. This consistency, combined with the fact that a "Top of the Mind" perspective is more enjoyable to be around, will eventually either persuade them to give it a try, or let you know that, at this time in their life, they may just be too frightened to trust anything but fear as a guide for what they believe. In this case, a "Top of the Mind" perspective of compassion would be a good choice for us.

CHAPTER 21

C³ Clarity, Confidence, & Creativity with People & Life

A s with the first part of the book, the LEAP model combined with the BRAIN model and the POWER model is designed to bring the C³ / "Top of the Mind" perspective to life, especially when life is about dealing successfully with others. Therefore, when we are able to go into any situation with...

- Clarity of purpose, and being clear as to how we want to define ourselves, and/or the statement we want to make about who we are. . .

- Clarity of our past habits and how beliefs, interpretations, and expectations drive everyone's emotions and behaviors . . .

- Clarity about the wisdom of serenity, or the value of gaining this neocortex perspective before attempting to become influential with others. . .

- Clarity about the energy that we are going to use in these situations (receptive before active), curiosity, empathy, and neocortex questions before problem-solving, and finally . . .

- Clarity about the value of our taking 100% responsibility for our ability to respond so that we don't need anything or anyone around us to change in order for us to practice this higher purpose, we will be more powerful.

One way to access this clarity is to put each of these steps in the form of a Neocortex question and use the BRAIN Model to ask the question and implement the answer as the graphic below illustrates.

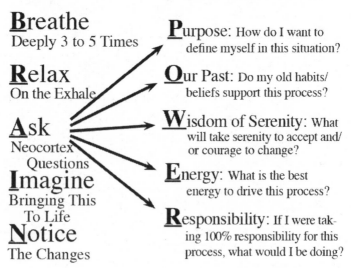

Breathe
Deeply 3 to 5 Times

Relax
On the Exhale

Ask
Neocortex
Questions

Imagine
Bringing This
To Life

Notice
The Changes

Purpose: How do I want to define myself in this situation?

Our Past: Do my old habits/ beliefs support this process?

Wisdom of Serenity: What will take serenity to accept and/ or courage to change?

Energy: What is the best energy to drive this process?

Responsibility: If I were taking 100% responsibility for this process, what would I be doing?

In addition, in order to deal with people effectively, we need to be clear about what I call, "The Four Whats:"

1. **What part of the brain are they coming from?** If people are in their brainstem, we don't want to give them data or just tell them to "calm down."

2. **What thought, emotion, or perspective is driving their reaction?** Again, in order to influence others, we must know what is influencing them!

3. **What about this perspective can we either agree with or at least understand?** One thing that is driving their resistance is their fear that we can't or won't see things from their perspective. We don't have to agree with them, but we must be able to at least understand why they are reacting the way they are to be influential.

4. **What neocortex question (meaning what question about the future and a solution) will help them shift from their brainstem to their neocortex?** In order for us to be influential, we must shift from a debate about the problem and the past (generally around "Who's right?") to a conversation about the future, because in the future, there is no blame or guilt, and we can craft a solution that has aspects of what is important to them, as well as, what is important to us.

In fact, if we combine the "Four What's" with the LEAP model, we have my six-step process for dealing successfully with others.

It begins with knowing what we want to Bring & Bring Out!

Step One: **Bring** - Begin by ensuring that we are coming from the clear, confident, and creative part of our brain, or the Top of the Mind. This means never engaging someone when we are feeling frustrated, anxious, angry, or resentful. Instead we must always know what we are starting, or the qualities and characteristics we want to *bring* to the situation in order to be successful.

Step Two: **Bring Out** - Be sure we are also clear about our highest purpose for them. What are the qualities we want to *bring out* in them, or the characteristics we want them to start versus focusing on what we want them to stop.

Step Three: **Listen and Learn** -
  A. What part of the brain are they coming from?
  B. What thought, emotion, or perspective is driving their reaction?

Step Four: **Empathize** - So that they no longer need to defend the righteousness of their perspective.

Step Five: **Ask** - Neocortex Questions which are questions about the solution and the future versus the problem and the past.

Step Six: **Problem-solve**. The last step!

As we become skilled in this process, we will then be able to interact more confidently with others, and access our most creative thoughts and ideas. In other words, we will be able to bring our best to life, and become more influential in our lives and in the lives of others.

Part IV

CHAPTER 22

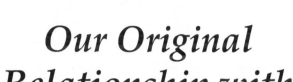

Our Original Relationship with Food and Weight

W eight, weight loss, and body image are understandably a big issue among students of the performing arts. One reason for this is that the industry tends to overemphasize looks in terms of how someone is evaluated for a role, and this reality (combined with society's bias of "thin equals good"), often results in young artists being very worried about their weight. In its most severe form, this worry can manifest as an eating disorder, but even if it is "just" a problem with body image, this perception can trigger stress and have us restricting our intake of food and obsessing about our weight in ways that are incongruent with the happiness, health, and peace of mind that we have decided are the most important things in our lives (or our Highest Purpose).

Of course, just hearing well-meaning adults tell you to stop obsessing, and/or don't worry about your weight is not helpful because (a) we are focusing on what we are supposed to be stopping versus starting, and (b) the implication here is that if we don't stop this worrying, something bad will happen (which triggers more worrying). Plus, as mentioned, there is this reality out there about what one "should look like" if one wants to be successful in the visual arts.

To deal with this dilemma, I suggest we look at the subject of food and weight from a "Top of the Mind" perspective, and start from the beginning. For example, babies are very good at regulating their intake of food. They respond not to some external standard of what they should look like or what everyone else is doing, but to an internal signal from their body. To put it simply, when they are hungry, they eat and when they are no longer hungry, they stop eating. Brilliant!

Notice how this differs from how most people relate to food. In today's world, people eat because it's time to eat, other people are eating, they have paid good money for the food, to keep from being hungry later, all sorts of reasons that have nothing to do with hunger. Children are taught to eat in order to get dessert, to please the person who cooked the food, because everyone else is eating (it's dinner time), because of all the starving people around the world, etc., again, reasons having nothing to do with hunger.

This means that somewhere between the time when we naturally related to food as babies and who we are today, we learned to eat or not eat in a way that is unnatural, and is all based upon external signals. Therefore, I suggest we return to this natural way of eating, and I further suggest that doing so will also allow our body to find its natural, healthy weight and allow us to stop dieting, eat anything we want, and maintain our healthy weight for the rest of our lives.

This perspective begins with the concept of **Purpose**, the first of the five steps (The POWER Model) that we have discussed so far in living "Life from the Top of the Mind." In other words, what is the purpose of food? I suggest that food has two purposes...one, to nourish our body and provide the energy we need to perform and do what we want, and two, it should be a pleasant experience. However, it shouldn't be the *only* pleasant experience in our lives, and further, its purpose isn't to deal with stress, or boredom, or provide comfort when we are anxious or sad.

Instead, eating should be a response to our

body giving us a natural, normal, healthy signal to begin to eat which is *hunger*. To be clear, hunger must come from the middle of our body. In other words, the true signal of hunger is felt as movement in our stomach because it is empty, and is generally only felt three and half, to five hours after we eat. It is not a thought that, "gee this would really taste good" or some desire for food.

Again, babies are very good at responding to this natural signal and when we are tasked with caring for a baby, we naturally feed it when it's hungry. In fact, can you imagine knowing that someone you love (a baby, for example) is hungry and NOT feeding him or her? Doesn't that sound almost abusive?

And yet, how often have we felt the signal of hunger but not eaten because we were afraid that there was no time to eat, or out of fear of getting fat? Unfortunately, this actually produces cortisol because the body thinks we are in a famine! Cortisol triggers the production of glucose because we need extra glucose for energy in a fight-or-flight situation. However, we are not in a fight-or-flight situation, and therefore, when we worry about food and/ or our weight, we are simply producing more and more glucose. Glucose is sugar. Sugar, when it's not burned off, turns to fat, which is what we were worried about in the first place. See the problem here?

The solution is to see our body not as the

problem, but as a significant part of the solution, and trust that the signal of hunger is a natural, normal, healthy signal to begin eating.

Now, our body will also give us a natural, normal, heathy signal to stop eating, but it is not feeling "full". There is actually a twenty minute lag between when your stomach is full and when your brain registers the feeling of "full." Therefore, *if you stop eating when you are full, you have been eating for at least 20 minutes longer than your body needs!*

The key to dealing with food and weight from a "Top of the Mind" perspective is to **use the same signal to stop eating that you used to start eating!** In other words, you start eating when you are hungry, and you stop eating when you are **no longer hungry!**

Unfortunately, few people know what being "no longer hungry" feels like, and therefore, this will take a bit of practice to master. The way to do this is again, only eat when you are hungry, and then as you eat, keep the question in mind, "Am I still hungry?"

The good news is that as we keep this new awareness in mind, our body will let us know when we are no longer hungry, and we can stop eating. Soon this will become a new habit, and you won't have to think about it. However, for a while it will require your purposeful attention.

Of course, I believe that we should have dessert at the end of every meal, and I also think the tendency to deny ourselves this pleasure is the reason why so many people find themselves eating entire cakes, pies, and quarts of ice cream at times. We feel deprived when we want something but don't get it, and therefore, when we finally give ourselves permission to have it, we are coming from a place of deprivation which triggers the desire to overeat.

Instead, I suggest we reject the deprivation model, and instead fashion a way of having dessert without gaining weight. Of course, we can't use the signal of hunger/no hunger because, at the end of the meal we won't be hungry.

Therefore I suggest we shift to the signal of taste. In other words, when we take the first bite of whatever dessert we have chosen, we rate it from 1 to 10 (with 10 being the best). If it isn't a 10, don't eat any more because the experience won't be worth the calories. However, the truth is that most desserts are a 10 so that is rarely an issue.

If the first bite is a 10, you savor the flavor, the sweetness, the texture, every aspect of the experience that is positive. Then you take the next bite. Because our taste buds have already started acclimating to the sweetness, this second bite will still be good but not as good as the first... say, a nine and a half. Now the next, maybe an 8, then a seven. When you get down to a 6, you stop eating. This way you always have the best part of the dessert (the part that tastes the best) but you never eat enough to produce weight gain.

Notice, I am not speaking of losing weight. In fact, I suggest that you never try to lose weight! There are several reasons for this statement. First we are programed to find what we lose ("Must be around here somewhere"). Second, the need to lose weight is driven by a concern, or worry about what will happen if we don't. This, like any concern or fear will trigger the production of cortisol, which triggers the production of glucose which if not burned off, turns to sugar and gets stored as fat.

Instead, I suggest that we go back to how we related to food as babies and work with our body to *find* its natural, normal, healthy weight. In fact, we can use the POWER model to support this process.

Purpose

We have already defined our purpose, allowing our body to find its natural weight by only eating when we are hungry and stopping when we are no longer hungry, just as we would want for someone we love.

Our Past/P.I.E.

Looking at our past and our piece of the P.I.E. (our Perceptions, Interpretations, and Expectations) lets us know how we came to think about food and weight, and the new beliefs/P.I.E. we will want to adopt in order to move forward in a most effective way.

The W̲isdom of Serenity

This is an important step, because in order for us to go forward in a positive frame of mind, we must be able to accept our body as it is. Now, we know that serenity is the precursor to acceptance, which is then the precursor to courage, wisdom, and change. One way to bring all these qualities to our relationship with food is to see our body as an excellent feedback mechanism. Its shape and weight at the moment are two pieces of good information about how we have related to food in the past. It will continue to be a good feedback mechanism as we change our relationship to food in the future... *if* we have the patience of serenity to allow this to happen.

The alternative here is a lack of acceptance which will trigger resentment, worry and anxiety, which triggers cortisol, glucose, sugar and fat. Instead, we want to accept what is today so that we can change our relationship with food and begin the process of transformation.

The E̲nergy We Choose to Drive This Process

The goal here is to ensure that we are using the energies of optimism and confidence to think about the process of change. Not only will this have us creating images of success, and thus maximizing the potential that we will succeed, it will have us triggering the neurotransmitters and endorphins that support the process.

Again, this is in contrast to the energies of worry, shame, and disgust, which do the opposite.

Responsibility

This final step in the POWER Model as it relates to changing our relationship with food and weight, is about taking charge of this process in a way that gives us total control. If you remember, I see responsibility as our "ability to respond." With respect to eating, this means that we need nothing to change externally for us to be successful. We don't need others to minimize our portions, or only offer us food when we are hungry or even believe in us to pull this off.

We also know that our "ability to respond" to food and weight in this new way will be a process. It's not about being perfect, just purposeful. Therefore, if we find ourselves eating in a way that is more about past habits versus how we want to be now and in the future, we just take that as good information and choose again.

The key, however, is that we take responsibility for these choices versus looking for someone else to blame.

The bottom line, is that being:
• **Purposeful** and aware of...
• **Our past**/P.I.E. and appreciating the...
• **Wisdom of serenity** and choosing the...
• **Energy** to guide this process, & taking 100%...

• **Responsibility** for our choices and our ability to respond... with respect to what we eat, and when we eat will serve us in our goal of creating a happy, meaningful, experience of life.

By the way, if you have noticed, I haven't spent much time talking about what we should eat. I have made this choice for two reasons. First, I'm not a nutritionist, nor a physician, and therefore don't have the training or expertise to make those types of recommendations. Second, I have found that always needing to eat "the right food" can also trigger resentment and a tendency to rebel.

In fact, in my own experience, I don't spend a lot of time and energy ensuring that my diet has a certain amount of one thing or another. I tend to go for what I think will taste good. That being said, I have noticed that as I have become more purposeful with *how* I eat, my choices of *what* to eat have gravitated towards the more healthy foods (salads, Greek yogurt with fruit, etc.)

Of course, I'm not saying that you shouldn't choose healthy foods (after all, isn't this what we would recommend to someone we love?). And further, if you are under a physician's care and have been medically advised to modify and/or restrict your diet/food choices due to a health condition, by all means, consult with your doctor before making any changes. I'm just saying that the need to eat only things that have been deemed "healthy" could result in that deprived feeling, and the tendency to splurge on sweets that I mentioned earlier.

Therefore, if I find myself truly hungry (I feel movement in my stomach and I haven't eaten for three and a half to five hours) and I want some pizza, pasta, or some other food that people on "diets"are forbidden to eat, I will tend to go ahead and enjoy those foods, until I'm no longer hungry of course, and then I go for dessert!

CHAPTER 23

Sex, Drugs, & Rock & Roll

O kay, this really doesn't have a lot to do with rock and roll, except for the fact that I was introduced to sex and drugs (in a way) while I was a rock drummer in a band around the age of 16. My band was playing a gig in Dallas, Texas, and we were traveling in an old school bus that was painted with psychedelic flowers on the outside, flat black inside with all the seats removed, and replaced with red carpet (yes, really).

After our gig, we went to an after-hours club in Dallas known as "The Cellar," where the music was first rate, and the waitresses wore only underwear.

One of them must have liked me, because she kept feeding me drinks, and the next thing I knew, it was morning, and I was waking up on the bus with her next to me, and a really nice case of gonorrhea to remember her by. Not my finest hour.

That being said, I do want to be clear that this isn't going to be a lecture on the dangers of drugs and sex, and how you should avoid them. As you know by now, my goal isn't to scare you into avoidance, but to give you as much information, and as many tools as possible to help you create the life you want.

With respect to sex, I can certainly see how this would be an important part of that life because it is so enjoyable, and because it is simply the most intimate way to connect with another person that I know of. As such, I'm a fan of using sex on purpose, in a way that creates a statement about the special-ness of that relationship, and in a way I would teach or recommend to someone I love.

Of course, the limbic system doesn't see it this way. To this part of our brain, sex is about survival of the species, and therefore, the more babies we make, the higher the percentage that one or more of those babies will survive to make more babies (hence, the tremendous power of lust). While this may have been necessary a long time ago, these days, I think it's safe to say that we don't have to go around copulating with as many people as possible to keep the human race alive.

So, how do we incorporate this very power-ful instinct/drive into our lives? How can we use sex versus sex using us? What role do we want it to play? How can we use sex in a way that makes a statement about who we are, and in a way we would recommend to someone we love?

For me, I like to use it to both signal that a relationship has reached a certain stage, and then as a way to continue nurturing that relationship. For example, in the past, when I met someone that I liked and we began to spend time together, I liked to have the level of intimacy mirror the development of the relationship. Not only does this allow the relation-ship to grow naturally, and allow each of the people in the relationship to participate in each milestone, it also allows us to enjoy each stage to its fullest.

For example, there is something special about the first touch of someone's hand and the first kiss. When these are allowed to happen in a natural pro-gression, the specialness of this increased intimacy informs the experience in a very memorable way. On the other hand, when we move straight from "Hello" to sex, we miss the specialness of the steps in between.

Plus, as we gradually bring intimacy into the relationship, we get to know the other person. Are they sensitive, giving, playful, adventuresome, kind, loving? Bottom line, what do we like and what do they like? Given that we are considering opening ourselves up to another person in this most intimate and vulnerable way, we want to know who they are, what their vision of sex looks like, and whether it is congruent with ours. If what turns them on involves pain (giving or receiving)? If this doesn't fit with what we like, we want to know this *before* we find ourselves in bed with them.

Plus, talking about what we both like can not only give us good information and lead to a more satisfying, meaningful, and enjoyable sexual experience, these sort of conversations are also arousing in and of themselves. Therefore, not only are you gathering very valuable information, you are building your sexual energy which will make the experience that much more intense.

I will leave it to you to determine what these steps are, and how long you want to spend getting to know someone before you open yourself up to them in this intimate way. I just encourage you to go into this aspect of your life the same way you have chosen to go into all of life... purposefully (or deliberately), in a way that makes the statement you want to make about who you are ("I am someone who uses sex to... deepen a relationship, get approval, escape from life, celebrate a meaningful connection, what?") and in a way you would teach or recommend to someone you love.

In this way, rather than being ruled by our limbic system's drive to make babies and propagate the species, or using sex as a drug to escape, or as a way of getting to know someone and / or make them like us, or being controlled by our fears that we are not enough, or that we are only valuable to someone if we can provide them with a sexual outlet... we are using the upper 80% of our brain and the POWER model to guide our sexual energy in a way that matches how we have chosen to live our lives. For example:

1. Purpose - This means we have made a purposeful decision about how we want to use sex and that this aspect of our lives is congruent with our Highest Purpose, or the qualities and characteristics we want to bring to life as a statement about who we are (loving, sensitive, playful, adventuresome, sensuous, trusting, open, caring, kind, etc.).

2. Our Past and Our P.I.E.

Of course, we know that we don't come to this time in our lives as blank slates. We have experienced things, and been told things in our past that have influenced our beliefs (Perceptions, Interpretations, and Expectations) about sex. To the degree that these experiences, beliefs, and our Piece of the P.I.E. are congruent with our highest purpose, then we need do nothing but continue to follow them as guides.

However, if some of our past experiences or what we have come to believe about this aspect of our lives are incongruent with this Higher Purpose,

then we want to ensure that we change our perceptions, interpretations, and expectations about this
powerful drive before we tap into its energy. For
example, if we have been sexually abused in the
past, this violation can have us (and especially our
limbic system) perceiving the act as dangerous, or
the only thing that people want from us.

By the same token, if we have learned that sex
is wrong or dirty, then we will have trouble trusting
our sexual desires, and this will set up an internal
struggle that can compromise our ability to trust
ourselves in other aspects of life.

The key here is to remember that so much of
how we see ourselves and our place in the world
was learned from the past. Our job, if we want to
become the captain of our own ship, is to determine
which of these beliefs, (Perceptions, Interpretations,
and Expectations) we want to hang on to and use as
guides, and which ones we want to change. When
we then become clear about what we want our new
beliefs (P.I.E) to look like, we can go into life confident in our ability to trust, and engage this powerful
aspect of life in a way that we can be proud of, and
in a way that improves the quality of our relationships.

3. The Wisdom of Serenity
This is about being accepting of ourselves
while we learn to be sexually skilled, and given that
earlier in the book I have spoken to the idea of seren-

ity being the precursor to acceptance, it is important to know how to bring both of these (serenity and acceptance) into play as we become more purposeful in this area of our lives. The truth is that simple lust or sexual energy doesn't create a meaningful, or even enjoyable sexual experience, and certainly not the one we have been lead to believe we are supposed to have by the media.

Instead, most people experience a bit of sexual awkwardness early in their lives which they often interpret to mean that there is something wrong with them or their partner. Unfortunately, this can have people doing things they really don't want to do (or taking drugs to suppress the anxiety) because they think that sex is always supposed to be easy and naturally wonderful from the beginning.

The truth is that as with any other skill, we get better at sex as we grow, learn, and mature. Therefore, we want to be gentle with ourselves (accepting) and not put expectations on ourselves or our partner that interfere with the loving, sensitive, and caring experience that sex can be.

4. The Energy

As always, this is about choosing love over fear, awareness over worry, excellence over perfection, and aligning our beliefs and behavior around sex with these more purposeful energies. Of course, this can be challenging because of the vulnerability that a sexual experience can trigger. However, this is one more reason for knowing the person with whom we are going to be sexual, because it's easier to trust and be open and vulnerable with someone we know well.

5. Responsibility

As you know, this is about our "ability to respond," and our willingness to take 100% responsibility for our choices around sex. This means we don't put ourselves in sexual situations that we wouldn't recommend to those we love. Nor do we acquiesce to others' demands or desires if they are incongruent with what we want in a sexual relationship.

Bottom line, if we want to be in charge of how we experience sex, we must be willing to play a major role in determining what that sexual experience will look like, and communicating that to our partner. If they share our vision, then that is good information. If not, this is also good information about whether this is a person with whom we really want to be vulnerable.

Drugs...

According to Wikipedia, a drug is, in the broadest of terms, a chemical substance that has known biological effects on humans or other animals. I'm going to go with that broad definition, and bypass the legal/illegal debate on certain drugs for the momment, to ensure that this doesn't come across as just one more adult telling you what you should and shouldn't do. (The only exception to this would be to acknowledge that often, the people who sell illegal drugs are not the kind of people we would want in our lives, nor do they tend to live a life that is congruent with what we would recommend to someone we love).

Instead, I would like to frame my perspective in a way that has the highest potential of being valuable to you, especially as it pertains to your creating joy in your life. This reminds me of a quote by Sidney Poitier from his book, "The Measure of a Man. He said:

"True joy is the difference between creating meaningful pleasure and just amusing ourselves to death."

Therefore, if true joy is important to you, I want to give you my best thoughts on how to create this way of being without the use of drugs. Why? because I don't like relying on some external stimuli to create my experience of life. I certainly don't want to give drugs the power to define me ("drugs make me happy.") Nor do I want to tie my joy to some stimuli that I have to get from someone else.

Now, remember, this isn't me going on an "anti-drug" rant. In fact, when I was getting a colonoscopy not so long ago, I was very grateful for the skill of the anesthesiologist and the drugs she used to ensure I didn't feel anything. Same thing for the dentist, and even the over-the-counter medication I take to eliminate the pain in my back from time to time.

No, what I'm talking about is the tendency for people to use drugs to create joy or pleasure in their lives (or to escape from their anxiety). I'm suggesting that this can be a problem because the act of taking a drug reinforces a belief that we don't have the ability to create joy or deal with stress on our own. It defines us as dependent, and in doing so, diminishes the belief that we have the ability to create the experience of life we want.

However, let's be clear. We all know that the reason people use drugs, at least in the beginning, is because they work! That is, they can make the user "feel better," at least for a while. This can be especially true if the user is feeling bad (anxious, fearful, worried, less than confident, etc.) prior to the drink, pill, or whatever. In other words, when people are in the brainstem and the chemical make-up of their body is more closely associated with stress and a perceived problem, drugs can either numb that anxiety or mask it with an artificial sense of confidence and/or pleasure.

This can be especially powerful when people find themselves haunted by the past, or obsessively worrying about the future. Drugs tend to numb both of those anxieties and provide an escape from these fears, and I know that some people are afraid that this is their only way of coping and/or the only way they can live in the present moment. Take, for example Sia's song "Chandelier:"

"Keep my glass full until morning light, 'cause I'm just holding on for tonight - I'm gonna live like tomorrow doesn't exist...

Like it doesn't exist."

Unfortunately, we also know that the solution can become the problem as we seek to deal with life by drugging ourselves into one state or another, and thus turn ourselves and our lives over to some external stimuli. Evidence the rats that keep pressing the bar that distributes cocaine until they literally die from starvation or exhaustion.

Therefore, I suggest we start from a position with which we all agree. In other words, I think we can all agree that drugs such as heroin or cocaine are not a good idea for anyone, and especially those who want to be at their most aware, and develop their talent to the fullest. I think we can also agree that using drugs (even alcohol and marijuana) to escape from our fears, self-medicate, or deal with stress and anxiety is also not something we would recommend to someone we love.

Therefore, what we are talking about is whether to use drugs socially or "recreationally" where no addiction issue or impairment is a problem... at a party, for example. To be fair, drugs (especially alcohol) are a part of our culture. Chances are, many of our parents used alcohol and didn't suffer any particularly negative consequences, and now marijuana is being legalized in state after state. This would understandably lead one to believe that "responsible" use of drugs shouldn't be a problem.

The problem, of course, is that, at the writing of this book, drinking is illegal for those under a certain age in all states, and recreational marijuana is illegal for everyone under 21 everywhere.

Now, many people argue that this shouldn't be the case and that because the law is stupid, there is no reason to obey it. And, because I'm not a proponent of "obedience" as a way of life, I'm not going to try to convince you to simply obey a law you don't agree with.

What I am going to suggest, however, is that there are other considerations here that might be more important to you. For example, from what I understand, getting into a really good BFA program is quite competitive. Chances are you really wanted this and were thrilled when you were accepted. I'm guessing that the experience of being in the program is very rewarding. If so, is a high at a party worth putting that at risk?

And what about your professors? One thing that I notice about performing and visual arts programs is that the students and professors can be quite close. Trust me, this isn't always the case in other departments. Also, from what I hear, this connection with your teachers is one of the most treasured aspects of the college experience. If so, is a high at a party worth putting that at risk?

Plus, there is the reputation of your professors within the university. Often when students (especially those in the performing and visual arts) get into trouble for drugs, other department heads interpret this to mean that the department is "out of control" and that the professors are doing a poor job. This judgement could exacerbated by the belief that the professors aren't being tough enough to begin with, and that the students and the professors are "too close." Regardless, this can affect future funding for the department, and how your teachers are percieved on campus. Is a high at a party worth putting that at risk?

Then there is your reputation with your professors. Chances are when you were admitted to the program you made an agreement that you wouldn't use drugs. It's possible that you may have seen this as just one more hoop you had to jump through, but to your professors, this was your word. Just like everything else we do, if we break this agreement it makes a statement about who we are.

We all know how nebulous the future is for artists, in general, and it's possible that one of the reasons you chose this program was because of the reputation and connections that your professors have with the professional performing and visual arts community. One of the things directors want to know before they cast someone to play a role is whether they are dependable... if they give me their word, will they keep it? The first person they are likely to ask is their friend (your professor) who just spent four years with you. Is a high at a party worth putting that at risk?

Bottom line, if we are using drugs to self-medicate, escape from our fears, or in a way we wouldn't recommend to someone we love, that needs to change. If we are using them to enhance our experience at parties, it's not worth putting the things we care more about at risk.

Therefore, I suggest we take charge of this aspect of our lives and use drugs in a POWERful way that is congruent with our Highest Purpose, or the statement we want to make about who we are.

For example:

1. Purpose - We have decided what purpose drugs play in our lives and we have chosen to use them in a way we would recommend to someone we love.

2. We understand that Our Past and our beliefs (perceptions, interpretations, and expectations) around drugs may not have been formed on purpose, but

they will definitely control our choices until we take control and change how we view the use of drugs.

3. The Wisdom of Serenity, which is about asking the questions, "What will we need serenity to accept with respect to our lives and drugs, and what will we need courage to change?" For example, it may take serenity to accept the fact that there will be times when we are feeling less than great, and we will be tempted to use drugs to deal with that feeling. If instead, we can bring a certain amount of serenity into the process (the BRAIN Model) this will allow us to accept this feeling at the moment (without having to self-medicate it away), and we can then begin to courageously look for ways to change the chemical make-up of our body (and therefore change the feeling) in a way we would recommend to someone we love.

And, of course, there is the courage to ask for help when we find that the idea of stopping on our own seems too overwhelming. This is where my having grown up with parents who were very involved with AA and Al-Anon has given me a tremendous amount of respect for those individuals who have the courage to ask for help, and for the people who help others reclaim their lives from drugs.

4. We choose the Energy we want to guide these choices, love over fear, courage over hopelessness, optimism over pessimism, awareness over

worry, etc.

5. And finally, our willingness to take 100% <u>R</u>esponsibility for our "ability to respond" with respect to how we use drugs in our lives. This means that, other than reaching out for help when needed, we don't require anything or anyone to change outside of us before we choose to take control of our lives.

Again, drawing from Sidney Poitier's quote, this is about creating "true joy" or the experience of "meaningful pleasure" versus just amusing ourselves to death. As artists, you probably have a better sense of what that true joy feels like because it's why you do what you do... and why you have chosen this path for your life.

How about we free our brain and body to serve the creation of this true joy in a way that gives us access to all of our clarity, confidence, and creativity, free from the influence of some external substance, and in a way that represents what is most important to us? In this way, we once again become the most powerful influence in our lives and are able to bring this influence into almost any situation... in a way, of course, that we would recommend to someone we love.

CHAPTER 24

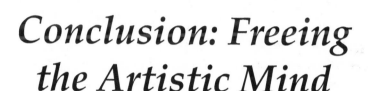

Conclusion: Freeing the Artistic Mind

If you remember, we began with a quote from Albert Einstein: *"Problems cannot be solved at the same level of awareness that created them"*. My hope is that you now have a new awareness of what is actually happening when we find ourselves reacting in old, less than purposeful ways. You also have the C-Cubed Model of Clarity, Confidence, and Creativity to support you in this process.

That being said, up to this point we have mostly been speaking of the third component of this model, *creativity*, as a verb, i.e., to create a more purposeful experience of life, we want to be coming from the most purposeful part of the brain. As an artist, however, there is another type of creativity that is essential to your success, and it is this creativity that I want to address in this final chapter.

Wikipedia defines creativity as: "a phenomenon whereby something new and in some way valuable is created." I like this because it differentiates between the process of learning a song, or lines in a play, and the experience of bringing those words/lyrics to life in a performance. The first is a very purposeful process, while the second (the performance) is more of an experience. In other words, while it is possible to will ourselves to learn lines and lyrics, we can't will ourselves to be creative, and this makes the state of creativity a bit more illusive.

Plus, we now know that old fear-based beliefs such as, "I'm not good enough," "I'm going to look like a fool," "I'm just setting myself up for rejection," will (if allowed to), minimize our creative abilities because they are taking up "brain space" that we need to support our creativity. The truth is that in order to create something new and valuable, we need access to our entire brain, and the good news is that most young artists have some sense of what this is like.

As we have discussed, chances are that there have been times in the past when you were "in the flow" (as it is called), caught up in the joy of performing, and as such, were not really thinking of how you "should be," or worrying about screwing up. In fact, it may have been experiences such as these that lead to your choosing the performing arts as a field of study and eventual career. It was certainly during these times that your entire brain (right and left hemisphere, brainstem, limbic system, and neocortex) was engaged in a way that resulted in your maximum creativity, and this will also be the case in the future.

You see, while we have been talking about the brain as separate parts in order to understand and influence our emotions and behaviors, the reality is that it is a very connected organ in which the whole is way more than the sum of its parts. This is especially true when it comes to creativity and, as an artist, understanding this will be critical to your success.

The good news is that everything you have learned in this book will be useful in this endeavor. That's because as you become increasingly skilled at defining who you are in a wide variety of circumstances (relationships, school, auditions, with friends), your confidence will increase as well. This clarity and confidence will then allow you to tap into all the colors of your creativity in greater depth, because those old, limiting, fear-based beliefs will no longer be holding you back.

Therefore, I suggest you continue to use life as a place to practice. In fact, there is one more quote from Albert Einstein that should be helpful in this practice. It says:

"There are only two ways to live your life, one as if nothing is a miracle & the other as if <u>everything</u> is."
Albert Einstein

One as if all of the negative events and people in our lives "make us" feel the way we do, and the other as if these situations provide a series of miraculous opportunities for us to define ourselves "on purpose," in a way that maximizes our clarity and confidence, and frees the creative, artistic mind to bring something new and valuable to life.

This has been my goal in writing this book... to give you all I know, and all my best thoughts on creating the life you want, and in doing so, I know I have given you a lot to remember. The good news is that the essence of each step exists in all the other steps as well. For example, if you go into a situation clear about your highest purpose, or how you want to define yourself, you will automatically be paying more attention to your beliefs, the wisdom of serenity, the energy you choose, etc. By the same token, if you are willing to take 100% responsibility for who you are and how you respond, you will also be more purposeful in terms of the energy/beliefs you choose, and what you practice. Therefore, if one particular step or concept resonates with you more than another, feel free to use it to guide your choices/practice, and you should be well-served.

For those of you who would like some support in this endeavor, or just wish to stay connected to the material, I invite you to go to my website (www.billcphd.com) and sign up for my free newsletter which is sent out each week and always contains one of my favorite quotes, as well as, several paragraphs about how to apply that quote to our lives. I'm now including a short video with this email, and I have saved all of my past quotes, comments, and videos on my website and my YouTube channel for you to access at your convenience. I also invite you to send me any thoughts you have about the material in this book, in that I always look forward to hearing how people are taking my concepts and applying them in their lives... and, I'm always looking for ways to make my ideas more helpful and easier to understand and implement for you, and young artists everywhere.

Until then . . . Enjoy, In Joy

The Top of the Mind Inventory™

For those of you who like to quantify the degree to which you are coming from your most productive part of your brain, I have created a short test, or inventory that should be helpful. Keep in mind, however, that unlike most instruments of this kind, the *Top of the Mind Inventory* does not attempt to get at what you "really think" by asking the same question in many different ways. Nor is there an attempt to keep one from skewing the results to make them "look good."

The thing to remember in taking this inventory is that all you are going for here is awareness. No one but you will see the results, and thus, this is not the time to worry about whether or not you come out with a "good score" (a brainstem concern, by the way). As the good Dr. Einstein said, "Problems cannot be solved at the same level of awareness that created them," and so I encourage you to use this instrument and your results as "good information" about what part of your brain is driving your thoughts, decisions, and emotions.

The Top of the Mind Inventory™
Created by Bill Crawford, Ph.D.

In response to the statements below, please choose one of these five responses:

Almost Always	Most of the Time	About 1/2 of the Time	Some of the Time	Almost Never
1	2	3	4	5

I tend to become frustrated, stressed, and/ or worried when...

1. I am stuck in traffic, or in a long line.

Almost Always	Most of the Time	About 1/2 of the Time	Some of the Time	Almost Never
1	2	3	4	5

2. I am faced with a deadline.

Almost Always	Most of the Time	About 1/2 of the Time	Some of the Time	Almost Never
1	2	3	4	5

3. I am auditioning for a part.

Almost Always	Most of the Time	About 1/2 of the Time	Some of the Time	Almost Never
1	2	3	4	5

4. I am late, or running behind schedule.

Almost Always	Most of the Time	About 1/2 of the Time	Some of the Time	Almost Never
1	2	3	4	5

5. I think about my past.

Almost Always	Most of the Time	About 1/2 of the Time	Some of the Time	Almost Never
1	2	3	4	5

6. I think about my present situation.

Almost Always	Most of the Time	About 1/2 of the Time	Some of the Time	Almost Never
1	2	3	4	5

I tend to become frustrated, stressed, and/or worried when...

7. I think about my future.

Almost Always	Most of the Time	About 1/2 of the Time	Some of the Time	Almost Never
1	2	3	4	5

8. Someone criticizes my work.

Almost Always	Most of the Time	About 1/2 of the Time	Some of the Time	Almost Never
1	2	3	4	5

9. I fail to live up to expectations.

Almost Always	Most of the Time	About 1/2 of the Time	Some of the Time	Almost Never
1	2	3	4	5

10. I evaluate my financial situation.

Almost Always	Most of the Time	About 1/2 of the Time	Some of the Time	Almost Never
1	2	3	4	5

11. Things don't go as planned.

Almost Always	Most of the Time	About 1/2 of the Time	Some of the Time	Almost Never
1	2	3	4	5

12. People don't do what they're supposed to.

Almost Always	Most of the Time	About 1/2 of the Time	Some of the Time	Almost Never
1	2	3	4	5

13. I make a mistake.

Almost Always	Most of the Time	About 1/2 of the Time	Some of the Time	Almost Never
1	2	3	4	5

14. I encounter a particular person, or type of person.

Almost Always	Most of the Time	About 1/2 of the Time	Some of the Time	Almost Never
1	2	3	4	5

15. I fail to reach a goal or achieve what I set out to accomplish.

Almost Always	Most of the Time	About 1/2 of the Time	Some of the Time	Almost Never
1	2	3	4	5

Now, simply determine your score by adding up your responses to each of the fifteen questions.

My Score _____

Now, let's plot your score on the brain map.

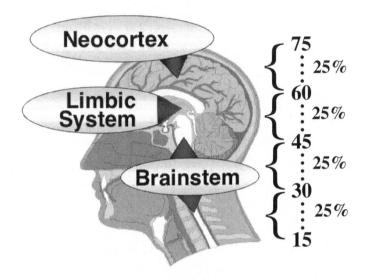

• A score in the upper 25% (60-75) means that you are coming from the "top of your mind" almost all of the time, and experience very little frustration, stress, or anxiety regardless of the situation. Whatever you are doing is working well, and thus the models in this book should reinforce what you already know, and provide support for you to continue to come from this "Top of the Mind" perspective.

• A score in the 45 to 59 range means that you operate from your neocortex most of the time. However, there are also situations where stress and/or frustration may get the better of you and throw you into the lower part of your brain. Given that you are coming from the neocortex most of the time, however, you can choose to interpret this as "good information," and apply the information in the book to the situation. Do this often enough, and you should soon find yourself moving into the upper 25%.

• A score in the 30 to 44 range means that you are experiencing much more frustration and stress than you like, and that you may feel unsure of what to do to fix what is wrong. This is because you are often trapped in the brainstem, and this lower part of the brain lacks the clarity, confidence, and creativity necessary to solve the problem. If you practice the models outlined in this book, however, you can begin to move up the scale and begin to increasingly engage your neocortex in the process of creating your experience of life. You might also consider engaging a professional to support you in this process so that you don't have to make this move all by yourself. Reaching out for help isn't a sign of weakness but of courage, and probably something you would recommend to someone you love.

• A score in the lower 25% of the scale (15 to 29) indicates that you probably feel worried, stressed, and anxious almost all the time. This is a tough place to be because neither of the two options available to you (fight-or-flight) will allow you to successfully address the problem. Plus, because you are trapped in the brainstem so much of your life, you are likely to feel trapped and undermined by life in general, and confused as to what to do. Here is where working with the BRAIN model will be an important first step, because you must initially allow the neocortex to regain some semblance of control in order to begin to operate from this higher-order thinking. Once this is done, the material in this book should be useful in helping you maintain this perspective, and with practice, you should be able to find yourself coming from the "Top of the Mind" on a much more regular basis. Getting support from a qualified mental health professional that you trust is even more important here, because the experience of being stuck in the brainstem is so frustrating and confusing. Chances are that you wouldn't want someone you cared for having to deal with this alone, and thus you will want to ensure that you have this kind of support as well.

Of course, this inventory is not designed to be an all-encompassing, diagnostic instrument, but simply a tool to help you identify what part of your brain is dominating your thinking. As you work with the models in this book, feel free to return and retake the test, and watch your score go higher as you access your higher -order thinking.

APPENDIX II

The BRAIN Model and Sleep

In my master classes, many people describe one of the problem areas in their lives as not being able to fall asleep or fall back to sleep if they wake up during the middle of the night. This is because few of us have been taught how to fall asleep, and, of course, because of our tendency to worry. For example, the way most of us "go to sleep" is just lay down and wait for it to happen. Unfortunately, when it doesn't, or when we wake up in the middle of the night, we begin to worry. We worry about things such as what we didn't do the day before or have to do tomorrow, etc. Soon we notice that we have been lying there "trying to go to sleep" for several hours, and we begin to worry about the fact that we will have to get up soon, and the cycle of stress is once again born and exacerbated.

Just as in other aspects of life, to break this cycle we must first understand what is happening to our body chemically in these sorts of situations. If you remember earlier, I told you that stress is actually just a series of chemicals released in our body, and how these chemicals (adrenaline, noradrenaline, and cortisol) can be beneficial in that they actually wake us up in the morning. The problem with falling asleep (or falling back asleep), however, is that when we are lying in bed worrying about the day before, the next day, and/or the fact that we haven't been able to fall asleep, *we are actually producing adrenaline and cortisol, or chemicals that are designed to wake us up!* No wonder we are less than successful.

The chemical we want to trigger instead is *melatonin.* In order to trigger the production of this chemical and achieve our desired state of restful sleep, we must first ensure that our neocortex is in control and our body is free of tension by breathing deeply three to five times, and saying the word "relax" on the exhale. Interestingly enough, this alone will begin to have us feeling more relaxed, and is a perfect prelude to sleep.

However, rather than just waiting for sleep to happen, we can speed up the process by asking the magic question: "How would I rather be feeling?" My guess is that words such as tired, sleepy, or drowsy might come to mind. Next, because any image we hold in our mind will trigger a chemical change in our body, we can imagine a time in the past when we were feeling really sleepy, when lying down and falling asleep was all we wanted to do. We further can remember how good it felt to lay down on the bed, how nice the sheets felt, etc. Then we could imagine what it would feel like right now if we were able to bring these feelings into the present. . .how nice the bed we are in feels, and how good it feels to be sleepy and tired. Finally, as we become more and more drowsy, we can imagine feeling this way in the future when just lying down begins to trigger a feeling of drowsiness and relaxation.

At this point, we will want to notice how much more sleepy and drowsy we are than when we started the process. Now it's just a matter of repeating the process (The BRAIN model) until we fall asleep.

Notice I'm speaking of falling asleep versus going to sleep. This is because we can't go to sleep! We can go to the store, or even to bed, but we can't go to sleep because it isn't a place we go, it is a state we fall into. Therefore, I encourage you to imagine being right on the edge of sleep and gently falling into this state.

The reason that all this works is that it focuses the brain on what you want versus what you are worried about, and because you are holding images of being sleepy in your mind, you produce "sleep" chemicals. Even if you need to go through the model several times, you will feel increasingly sleepy each time you do, and eventually you will fall asleep.

By the way, for those of you who want to become skilled at falling asleep in general, there are a few things you can do to develop this skill. First, you must be willing to go to bed at approximately the same time each night. This will have your body expecting sleep at this time, and cooperating with you by beginning to produce "sleep chemicals" around this hour of the evening. You will also want to make sure that you do the same things each night before you go to sleep in approximately the same sequence (brushing your teeth, taking a hot bath, reading a sleep-inducing book, etc.) because this will also trigger the production of these chemicals.

When I say a "sleep-inducing book," what I mean is one that has you producing endorphins versus adrenaline. While I am a fan of certain works by Stephen King, I don't recommend reading this sort of book before you go to bed. Not only will it produce adrenaline and keep you awake, it will most likely influence your dreams so that you keep producing stress chemicals throughout the night and wake up less than rested.

Instead, I encourage you to choose all aspects leading up to sleep in a very purposeful manner. Instead of looking at what time you "have to" go to bed and wake up. I suggest you decide how much sleep you would like to give your body (what will allow you to draw upon your energy and bring this to your art? What would you recommend to someone you love?). You then choose what time you *want to* get up (so that you have plenty of time to get ready in a relaxed way) and count backwards until you find the time you *want to* go to bed.

Notice how different this process is from what most people do? Unfortunately it's this "have to" mentality that produces resentment and rebellion. Ever since we were children, we have been resisting "bed time," and now that we are on our own, part of us wants to stay up all night just because we can! While this is understandable, it doesn't serve us if we want our body to be the reservoir we draw upon for our energy and creativity (a tired artist is a limited artist).

Plus, lack of sleep actually triggers the production of cortisol, which we now know works against us in so many ways. What we want to trigger is melatonin, and just as the ringing of a bell triggered Pavlov's dogs to salivate,so can everything you think and do in the evening trigger the production of melatonin, and support your goal of getting a good night's sleep, waking up rested, and being ready to bring your highest purpose to life.

Appendix III

Managaing Our Life and Time

Managing one's time is an issue that almost all college students struggle with, and especially those in the performing and visual arts. This is understandable because chances are, prior to college, your choices about how you spent your time were limited. In other words, you had to go to school... and then there was homework, and other things you had to do at home. Therefore, the only times you were in charge of your life were when you were working on your art or spending time with friends.

Unfortunately, in college, many students either rebel against all those years where they were told what to do by making "partying" their major, or they turn college into another series of "have to's," where they still feel that they have little to no choice in how they spend their time.

Neither of these options is a good idea. Instead, I suggest that you take charge of this area of your life, just as this book helps you take charge of your emotions and behaviors. To do this, we must first remove the word "have to" from the conversation, because it means that you have no choice, and it almost always breeds resentment. Plus it's not accurate. In fact, I suggest that there are only three things in life we "have to" do. We have to be born (we have no choice in that), we eventually have to die (again, we don't have the choice of living forever), and we have to live until we die. Everything else is a choice.

Given what you have learned about the brain from reading this book, you now know that purposeful choice about who we are and how we live our lives comes from the upper 80% of the brain, or the "Top of the Mind." And, frankly, there is no more important choice than how we spend our time, because it really means how we create our life. Therefore, I suggest we make these choices more purposefully, and in a way we would recommend to someone we love.

Of course, I understand that a part of you may be responding to this suggestion with, "Yeah right! Have you seen the amount of work they give us? And that doesn't even take into account all the extra work we have to do in the evening with classes, rehearsals, performances... How are we supposed to get all of this done?"

The answer is... it's possible that you can't.

Now, this may not an answer that many will say out loud because they are afraid that it will be taken as an excuse for some to slack off and not do their best. However, the truth is that the professors in all your classes do not get together and look at the work that they are cumulatively assigning to determine whether it is a good idea (or even feasible). This means that you must be able to prioritize, which is really what time/life management is all about. In other words, we only have so much time on the planet, and devoting that time to what is most important is a skill we all would be well-served to develop. In some ways, you are ahead of the game, because you have already determined that your art is an important aspect of your life, and therefore, worth your time. However, that still leaves other aspects of life that must be viewed from a purposeful perspective in order for you to be successful.

To be clear, unlike other time management programs, I'm not going to suggest that this is accomplished by dividing your day into smaller and smaller chunks of time, and micromanaging your scheduling process. Instead, just as I have brought you new information with respect to dealing with anxiety, I want to bring you a new perspective on managing your time/life so that you get the most from your college experience, and learn a skill that will support you in getting the most out of life.

Time/Life Management From the Top of the Mind

Basically, this process is about making purposeful decisions with respect to how you spend your time/life from the upper 80% of your brain, and in a way that is congruent with your highest purpose. Once this decision has been made, the next step is putting it into practice, and finally, fine-tuning the process by noticing what works and what doesn't. Of course, this assumes that you have become clear about your highest purpose, or what is most important in your life. In Chapter Nine, I talk about this concept more specifically, however, for now, it can be as simple as your decision to get a degree in the arts. Think back to that time before you actually started the program, when you were applying to different schools, going to auditions, etc. Chances are you were told that this degree requires a greater demand on one's time than other majors, right? In other words, you were informed that in addition to your normal classes, you will be spending time in master classes, rehearsals, performances, etc., and that this will require that you become skilled at managing your time. Isn't it fair to say that being in the arts was so important to you that you eagerly agreed to do whatever it took, and sincerely believed in your commitment to this choice?

Now that you have some idea of what this looks like in terms of time management, are you still committed? If not (meaning being in the arts is not important enough to become skilled in time management) then get out now! Change to a more traditional major that will allow you to go class during the day and do your homework at night. However, if being in this program and doing what you love is still so important that you would do almost anything to follow this dream, then this book, and specifically this appendix, are designed to give you the tools you need to master this skill. Just one thing...Chances are you will be better at this as "time" goes by, so be sure to be gentle with yourself in the early stages. Remember, just as with everything else, this isn't about being perfect, just purposeful.

The aspect of our lives that I suggest we look at first is sleep. Unfortunately, many students see this through the eyes of an adolescent who is sick of being told when to go to bed! Therefore, they stay up (because they can!) until they fall asleep, and resent the hell out of the fact that they "have to" get up to make an early class. Clearly not a "Top of the Mind" perspective. Instead, I suggest we shift from an adolescent to a more purposeful adult perspective, and make a decision on how much sleep we want, or how many hours of sleep will allow us to enjoy our life and bring our best to our art. This goes back to the question you answered in Chapter Nine, "What is my highest purpose?" or, "What are the qualities and characteristics that I want to bring to life?

As you may remember, most people respond with adjectives such as happy, engaged, loving, confident, creative, etc. Great answers, to be sure, but feel free to refer to your list, because this not only represents who you are at your best, but a way of being that makes life the most meaningful, and is the most enjoyable. So, now the question is, how many hours of sleep will support this way of being? Notice how this is very different from asking "when do I have go to bed?" and/or, "when do I have to wake up?"

If you have determined that 7 to 8 hours of sleep is congruent with your highest purpose, then you want to ask, "What time would I like to wake up? If I have chosen to be in class at a certain time (notice no "have to's" here, you signed up for this class), what time to I want to wake up to make the time between waking and getting to class congruent with my highest purpose? Or, if my goal is to create my life in a way that is the most enjoyable and meaningful, (including the time between when I wake up and my first class), what time to I want to wake up to enjoy getting ready and having something to eat?"

Can you see where we are going here? No longer will your precious time/life be a means to an end (i.e. how late can I sleep and still make it to class?), but instead you will begin your day creating your life on purpose. You have chosen how many hours you want to sleep, and chosen what time you want to wake up so that the time between waking and class is enjoyable and congruent with your highest purpose. Can you see how this can set you up for a more enjoyable day?

Of course, the timing of your first class is a choice as well. In other words, you have chosen this program because you want this degree. You have also agreed to, or chosen, the process of matriculating through classes in order to get you what you want. You have agreed to take certain classes within a four-year period, but when you take these classes is, to some degree, up to you. Are you a morning person? If so, an eight o'clock class might be perfect. If not, make your choices accordingly.

Next, you want to choose how you spend your time/life in class. This choice will be easier in your arts classes because it's what you love to do, and these classes are generally taught by people you enjoy being with. However, it is common for young artists to look at their "core" courses as necessary evils that they must tolerate to get their degree. While this is understandable, I suggest it is incongruent with the experience of life you want to create, and therefore deserves to be looked at in a more purposeful manner. For example, what if you were taking the course to prepare for a role? You want to get a basic foundation in the subject (history, math, English, etc.) so that you can draw on this knowledge as you rehearse for the role and when you are performing. How would this influence your experience in class?

I suggest that this is exactly what you are doing. In other words, you want to stock your neocortex, or "the library of your mind" with a wide variety of resources from which you can draw as an artist. And, going into your core classes with this intent will allow you to enjoy the experience in a way that is congruent with this goal.

After your morning classes, you will want to get something to eat, because, like sleep, eating is a foundational component of your ability to access the energy and creativity that you will want to draw upon as an artist. The truth is that when we are hungry but don't eat, our body starts to produce cortisol and other stress-related chemicals that throw us into the lower 20% of the brain. Given that this is where our anxiety, frustration, and memory lapses reside, it's not a place that is congruent with bringing our best to our art. Therefore, you want to fuel your instrument (your body) in a way that allows you to engage your art from a fulfilled versus a depleted perspective.

Next, you go into your afternoon classes (as if you were researching a role) and afterwards, have something to eat around dinner time so that you can go into your evening activities (the reason you are in the program in the first place) excited and engaged. Of course, students in more traditional majors have this time to work on their out-of-class assignments. However, you have chosen a different path. There are rewards in this choice in that the time you spend learning about your art will be meaningful and enjoyable (this can't always be said for other disciplines). However, along with this reward is the reality that you will want to be more purposeful with your time.

Therefore, this requires that you avoid trying to get all of your out-of-class assignments done after rehearsals or performances. Chances are you will be exhausted at that time, and forcing yourself to stay up to 2 a.m. or later "getting everything done" (which means you will only get six or less hours of sleep) will interfere with your ability to draw upon the energy and focus required of a successful artist.

Part of this new way of thinking about time / life requires that you shift from the "high school" model of classes to the college model. In high school, you went to class from morning to late afternoon, with little to no break. The evenings were supposed to be when you did your homework, and weekends were when you focused on everything but school.

In college, however, there will likely be days when you don't have a morning or afternoon class, or at the very least, you will have an hour to hour and a half break between classes. These are the times you want to devote to reading and other assignments that students in other disciplines do at night. It will also allow you to spend some of your evening time relaxing and connecting with friends, which is certainly an important part of a joyful/meaningful life. The same goes for weekends. Unlike high school, weekends represent a resource versus an escape, and therefore, if you set aside some of your time on the weekends to do the work that most other students do at night, you will be making the most of your time while enriching your life (more on what this might look like later).

So, back to the idea that you can't do it all (no one can) and the question of, "How will I know whether I am doing as much as I can and what to prioritize?" The answer is, you create your days on purpose in the way we have discussed, getting the amount of sleep you have chosen, and using a certain percentage of your "off" time (time when you are not in class or rehearsals) to do as much as is doable.

For example:
• If you have about three hours available after evening classes/rehearsals before you go to bed (finish

around 10 p.m., go to bed at around 1 a.m.), that adds up to around 15 hrs. (3 X 5 days = 15 hrs)

• And... you have at least eight or so hours available during the day over a week's time (which means you have at least one three hour block and a couple of hour and a half blocks, with some shorter time periods thrown in). (8 hrs.)...

• And... you have around 15 hours available on a normal weekend day (9 a.m. to 12 p.m., or 10 to 1 a.m. each weekend day) (15 X 2 days = 30 hrs)...

How do you want to spend this time (around 53 hours) in a way that is congruent with your highest purpose?

Let's say that you want to set aside around two hours a day during the week, and around 10 hours on the weekend to be with your friends, relax, etc., (or some combination of weekday and weekend time allocation). And, let's say we allocate about an hour each day for getting to and from campus, going from class to class, and another hour and a half per day for eating. If so, this still leaves around 21 to 22 hours a week for you to "get things done." This should be plenty of time to devote to all of your outside assignments, including those in your major.

Do you see how this is different from high school? You are identifying time during the day and the weekend, and using that time more purposefully than students in other majors because being an artist is this important to you. If you do this and you still can't get everything done, you start prioritizing.

Of course, you put your classes in your major first, that's why you are here. After that, once again, the question is, "What do you want to put in your neocortex library, and how much time do you want to devote to that process?" The truth is that all class work and homework is about learning, and not about a grade. Choose what you want to learn, and if you are choosing to spend your time/life on purpose (while maximizing the time spent in the upper 80% of the brain by using what you have learned in this book), you will be surprised at how much you can accomplish.

Of course, if you are in the Honor's College or on some sort of academic scholarship, then it will be important to pay some attention to your GPA. However, again, if you are willing to choose how you create your time/life in this purposeful way, the chances are very high that you will be fine. However, if after doing everything we have talked about, you are not fine, meaning that, you are doing your best (getting enough sleep, using your off time purposefully, etc.) but still falling behind, talk to your advisors. That's what they are here for, and often, they can spot the problem and offer solutions that have been honed over years of helping students succeed.

The thing that you want to keep in mind is

why you chose this path in the first place, and how important a career in the arts is to you. If it is still as important as it was when you got into the program, it is important enough to become skilled at using your time in the most purposeful way. One more thing…it will be a good idea to lay this out visually (either on your computer or a calendar) so that you can begin to see all the time that is available to you, and therefore use that time in a way that matches what is important to you.

The bottom line is that to be successful in this new environment (college) and in this course of study, you will want to assume control and becoming the most powerful person in your life (about time, don't you think?). And, as Voltaire said, "With great power comes great responsibility" (By the way, the person who stayed up all night and was late to class thinks Spiderman is the source of this wisdom). The key to wielding this power and responsibility in ways that are congruent with your highest purpose is to practice making purposeful choices in a way that defines who you are and in a way that you would recommend to someone you love. In this way, we own the role of "Chooser" in our lives, and the love of who we are and what we do becomes our energy of choice.

APPENDIX *IV*

Dealing With Loss and Grief

"All connections are infused with dreams of what is possible in the future. Thus, when we lose something or someone important to us, we aren't just grieving the loss, we are grieving the shattered dream."
~ Bill Crawford

As a psychologist and someone who has experienced loss firsthand (both of my parents died of cancer within about six months of each other when I was 21), I have come to understand that the natural, normal, healthy reaction to loss is grief. Unfortunately, our western culture doesn't seem to see it this way. Possibly, because of this lack of vision, or because grieving can be so intensely emotional, we try to avoid it and/or describe the feelings associated with the experience of grieving in rather pejorative terms. For example, we call it "breaking down, falling to pieces, losing it, becoming a basket case," etc., and thus we find it hard to move through this process when we experience a loss.

I know that this was my experience when I lost my parents. Being a male raised in the piney woods of Northeast Texas, I thought that the way to deal with grief was to resist feeling anything, and so, when faced with the loss of my parents (and given that I was an only child in my family), I shut down and tried to feel nothing. Unfortunately, not only was I successful in this resistance, I received a lot of support for this position. People would come up to me and congratulate me for "doing so well" and "being so strong." Little did they know that I had shut down altogether, and was just going through the motions.

Finally, after years of denial, I entered a master's program in psychology that had the wisdom to insist that the students deal with their issues before they were let loose on the public. This requirement turned out to be a blessing in disguise, because it allowed me to get in touch with these long-repressed emotions in a safe place with people that I trusted.

As a result, I finally began to open up and allow myself to feel the emotions that had been buried for so long...and a very strange thing happened.

For the first time in my life, it felt really, really good to feel really, really bad.

You see, when I decided to feel no pain after the loss of my parents, I also had unwittingly shut off my connection to my love for them as well. Thus, when I was willing to open up to the pain and allow it to be a reflection of my love, I was able to give the experience of grieving a sense of purpose and meaning. The tears became a testimony to my love for the two people who had given me life.

I also noticed that I was not only grieving the loss of my parents, but also what would never be. As I mentioned, I was only 21 at the time of their death, and was just beginning to reconnect with them after my "teenage independence" phase. Not only was that reconciliation cut short, but I realized that they would never see their grandchildren, never see me earn my Ph.D., and I would never have the opportunity to give to them as they had given to me.

This "Shattered Dream" concept (developed by Chicago psychologist, Ken Moses) has come to be a major component in my work with others who have experienced a loss, and it is one I suggest you adopt on your journey from college student to adult. Whether grieving the loss of a relationship, a loved one, a job, a pet, or even just the discovery that what we thought was going to happen will never come to pass, what we are all grieving is a shattered dream. Plus, since the dream, or our vision of the future is always perfect, always about hope and what we see as possible, the resulting grief reflects the depth of this pain.

Ken Moses is the previously-mentioned Chicago psychologist who has done some excellent work in this area, not only in framing the experience of loss and grief in terms of a shattered dream, but also in understanding the value of the process itself. Here is a quote I adapted from his writing:

"Grieving is not the problem, it's part of the solution. It is an unlearned, self-sufficient process that helps us to move from the past to the future, from inaction to action...
from shattered dreams to more
purposeful dreams based upon
who we really are and
what we can create."
~ Adapted from Ken Moses

As with my other ideas and philosophies on dealing with stress, frustration, anger, etc., the first thing I feel we need to understand is how the experience of grieving is tied to the physiology of our body. For example, most people know that we have two nervous systems: the sympathetic and the parasympathetic. The sympathetic nervous system is designed to gear us up to be able to fight or flee when faced with a threat or trauma of some sort. The parasympathetic nervous system is designed to bring us back to normal after facing this sort of trauma (such as loss). What many people don't know, however, is that one of the functions of this parasympathetic nervous system is the stimulation of the tear glands! Thus, crying (and the experience of grieving, in general) isn't in the way... it is the way! It's our parasympathetic nervous system kicking in to help us deal with the loss, return to "normal," and go on with life.

As mentioned earlier, this unfortunately isn't how our culture views the experience, and as a result, we are likely to find ourselves blocking the very process that is designed to help us heal and move on.

This is where Dr. Moses does an exceptional job of helping us see these emotions for the natural, normal, and even healthy "feeling states" that they are. Elizabeth Kubler-Ross was very instrumental in helping us normalize the experience of grieving early in the 1970's by describing the experience as a series of five stages (denial, anger, bargaining, depression, and acceptance). Although she did note that not everyone will go through each stage, or in this order, the fact that she defined her model as a series of stages has lead many to believe that this is what should happen. The problem with this assumption is that, as anyone who has experienced a loss knows, we don't move smoothly from one stage to another until we arrive at acceptance.

Dr. Moses, on the other hand, defines these stages as "seven feeling states of grieving," versus "five stages of grief," and I have found this alternate perspective to be very helpful. We might start with shock and denial, but then we might feel (in no particular order) confusion, anxiety, anger, fear, depression, and even guilt. Further, we can easily find ourselves re-experiencing these feeling states as they seem to wash over us much like a wave in the ocean. In fact, as with a wave, if we try to fight it, we will be unceremoniously up-ended, tossed around, and eventually thrown to the bottom. If, however, we are willing to let the wave roll over us, surrender to its natural, gravitational forces, and avoid trying to fight the experience, we can come out on the other side feeling a little lighter, and more free.

However, in order to do this, we must first see thoughts and feelings associated with grieving, not as the problem, but part of the solution . . . as our parasympathetic nervous system kicking in to help us deal with the trauma of loss. Next, we must understand why the loss affects us in this profound way… we are grieving not just the loss of a person or situation (job, relationship, etc.) we are also grieving a shattered dream. Plus, we are also very likely grieving any past shattered dreams that we resisted grieving at the time of the loss.

One way to help with this process of moving through the feeling states of grieving is to give them meaning. For example, Dr. Moses speaks of how shock and denial (generally the first of the feeling states) allow us to retreat into ourselves so that we can begin to marshall resources to deal with the loss. In other words, the reason it initially feels too overwhelming to deal with the loss is because it is actually too overwhelming! What is needed is a time of numbness so that we can create internal and external resources to help us face and accept what seems unacceptable. Anger and anxiety then move us from inaction to action, and help us begin to establish the kind of boundaries we need at times like these . . . boundaries that allow us to take care of ourselves versus always being so concerned about the needs of others that we put ourselves last on the list.

As mentioned earlier, crying can also be given a purpose. Instead of it being a sign of our failure to cope, or what we must hide to avoid making others uncomfortable, it can be a behavioral representation of our love for what or who we lost, and even a statement we make about ourselves of which we can be proud, i.e., I am a person who cares deeply, and when I lose someone or something that is important to me, I will feel sad. The alternative would be to feel nothing, which would either be a denial of what I truly felt (out of fear), or some sort of inability to feel natural, normal, healthy emotions.

When working with people who are grieving (or when grieving myself), I recommend allowing the tears to flow all the way down our cheeks and even drip onto our clothes, versus stopping them cold with a tissue at the edge of our eyes the way most people do. I encourage people to see their tears as "liquid love," or as a way to connect to and even celebrate our love for who or what we have lost. Then we can allow the wave to sweep over us, cleanse us, and even begin to wash away the pain. Anyone who has ever had a "good cry" knows this feeling. We surrender to the emotion, temporarily "losing control," and the natural, normal, healthy experience of grieving takes us to a new place... a place where the pain is not quite as bad, and yet the memory of the lost love is still as strong, or maybe even stronger because now we have learned to feel the love through the pain and give them both new meaning...a place where we move from the past to the future, from inaction to action, from shattered dreams to more purposeful dreams based upon who we really are and what we can create.

As a client I had the privilege to work with once said: "Tears are a river that takes us to places we've never been." Here's to our willingness to allow the current of that river to take us to a new place where loss is painful but not debilitating, because we have learned the art of grieving the shattered dream.

I would imagine that this would be especially important to students in the performing and visual arts for several reasons. One, moving others with your art is what you do. If you do not allow yourself to be moved, out of fear of the depth of the emotion or some other reason, then what you are practicing is avoidance. This reminds me of a quote that came to me when I was working with a client that says, "When our purpose becomes avoidance, our life becomes a void." When we are unwilling to dive into to the feelings of grieving and feel them with purpose and passion, what we create is a void which leaves us void of the emotions necessary to bring our art to life when sadness or any of the "feeling states" (anger, confusion, anxiety, fear, depression, guilt, etc.) is what is called for.

In addition, being able to grieve in this more purposeful and effective manner may serve you in other ways. For example, unlike a lot of people who are dealing with loss, as a performing artist, you may not have the ability to withdraw from life until you feel better. You may have a rehearsal, photo shoot, or performance coming up, and because so many other people are involved, you can't just bow out. However, if you are willing to become skilled at letting these natural, normal, healthy emotions wash over you (again, like a wave), it is likely that you will move through the wave quicker, and be ready to perform on the other side.

As with everything else in this book, the key here is to engage this aspect of life with clarity about the value of the process, gain confidence in our ability to move through the process in a healthy way, and develop creativity in how we give the experience meaning and purpose. Bottom line, I suggest we take the quote I have adapted from Ken Moses to heart, and make it our mantra with respect to grief and loss: "Grieving is not the problem, it's part of the solution. It is an unlearned, self-sufficient process that helps us to move from the past to the future, from inaction to action... from shattered dreams to more purposeful dreams based upon who we really are and what we can create."

APPENDIX V

Recommended Reading

If you have enjoyed this book and want to continue along this path, you might be interested in reading some of the works that have served as a foundation for much of what I know and believe. I want to take this opportunity to thank all of the authors listed below for taking the time to put their best thoughts down on paper so that others could learn and grow from their wisdom.

Bach, Richard. *Jonathan Livingston Seagull*. New York: Avon Books, 1970

Bach, Richard. *One*. New York: William Morrow & Co., 1988.

Bach, Richard. *Bridge Across Forever*. New York: William Morrow & Co., 1984.

Bach, Richard. *Illusions*. New York:
  Dell Publishing Co., 1977.

Bach, Richard. *Running From Safety*. New York:
  William Morrow & Co., 1994.

Benson, Herbert, M.D. *Timeless Healing: The Power
  & Biology of Belief*. New York: Scribner, 1996.

Covey, Stephen. *The 7 Habits of Highly Effective
  People*. New York: Simon & Schuster, 1989.

Dyer, Wayne. *Your Erroneous Zones*. New York,
  Funk & Wagnalls, 1976.

Goleman, Daniel. *Emotional Intelligence: Why It Can
  Matter More Than I.Q*. New York:
  Bantam Books, 1995.

Ornstein, Robert. *The Roots of the Self: Unraveling
  the Mystery of Who We Are*. Harper Collins,
  New York, 1995

Seligman, Martin, Ph.D. *Learned Optimism*. New
  York: Simon & Schuster, Inc. , 1990.

Wesbrooks, William, *Dramatic Circumstances: On
  Acting, Singing, and Living Inside the Stories
  We Tell*. Hal Leonard Performing Arts
  Publishing Group, 2014

About the Author

In addition to holding a doctorate in Counseling Psychology from the University of Houston, Dr. Crawford is a licensed psychologist, author of five books, organizational consultant, and speaker. Over the last 30 years, he has created over 3600 presentations for such organizations as Sprint, The American Medical Association, PBS, Texas State University, Carnegie Mellon, and Rider Universities, The Musical Theater Educator's Alliance (MTEA), The Relativity School, as well as, many other organizations and professional associations, both nationally and internationally. In addition, his two PBS specials have been seen by over 15 million people, and he has been quoted as an expert in such diverse publications as The New York Times, Entrepreneur, The Chicago Tribune, Self Magazine, The Dallas Morning News, The Huffington Post, and Working Mother, just to name a few.

For more information contact Dr. Crawford at:
Email - drbill@billcphd.com
Phone - 832-722-6147 or 1-800-530-8550
Website - www.BillCrawfordPhD.com

Made in the USA
San Bernardino, CA
16 August 2017